Sadlier PHONICS

LEVEL A

Jane M. Carr   Joanne M. McCarty

Patricia Scanlon   Anne F. Windle

Program Consultants

Grace R. Cavanagh, Ed.D.
Principal, P.S. 176
Board of Education
New York, New York

Vilma M. Vega, Ed.D.
Elementary Curriculum Supervisor
Hillsborough County Public Schools
Tampa, Florida

Patricia N. Grant
Director, Early Childhood Program
Sacred Heart School, Vailsburg
Newark, New Jersey

Donna A. Shadle
Kindergarten Specialist
St. Paul Elementary School
North Canton, Ohio

Eleanor M. Vargas
Resource Specialist Teacher
Los Angeles Unified School District
Los Angeles, California

Deborah A. Scigliano
First Grade Teacher
Assumption School
Pittsburgh, Pennsylvania

Sadlier-Oxford
A Division of William H. Sadlier, Inc.
New York, New York 10005-1002

Advisors

Stephanie Hart Brazell
Kindergarten/First Grade Teacher
Thousand Oaks, California

Sr. Paul Mary Janssens, O.P.
Principal
Aurora, Illinois

Sue Pecci
First Grade Teacher
Winter Springs, Florida

Debra L. Bates
Kindergarten/First Grade Teacher
Cleveland, Ohio

Damaris Hernandez-Reda
Assistant Principal
New York, New York

Sr. Dawn Gear, G.N.S.H.
Principal
Lilburn, Georgia

Mary L. Brown
Kindergarten/First Grade
Multi-Age Teacher
Chillicothe, Ohio

Theresa A. Kenney-Martinez
First Grade Teacher
Pomona, California

Anita Shevette
Kindergarten Teacher
Pomona, California

Sr. Paulette Marie Gregoire, R.J.M.
Principal
Fall River, Massachusetts

Noelle Deinken
Kindergarten Teacher
Thousand Oaks, California

Mary Lee Gedwill
Second Grade Teacher
North Olmstead, Ohio

Angela L. Stankiewicz
Principal
New Bedford, Massachusetts

JoAnne Nardone, Ed.D.
Program Review Specialist
New York, New York

Sr. Francis Helen Murphy, I.H.M.
Editorial Advisor
Immaculata, Pennsylvania

Rosemarie Valente
Second Grade Teacher
Newark, New Jersey

Laura A. Holzheimer
Title 1 Reading Teacher
Grades 1 – 3
Cleveland, Ohio

Sophia Finger, Ed.D.
Assistant Principal
New York, New York

Kelly Johnston Hackett
Instructional Technology Consultant
Orlando, Florida

Karen Jalowiec Losh
Fort Wayne, Indiana

Acknowledgements

William H. Sadlier, Inc. gratefully acknowledges the following for the use of copyrighted materials:

"Good Books, Good Times" (text only) by Lee Bennett Hopkins (Editor). Selection reprinted by permission of HarperCollins Publishers.

"Parades", (text only) from MY DADDY IS A COOL DUDE AND OTHER POEMS by Karama Fufuka. Used by permission of Dial Books for Young Readers, a division of Penguin Books USA Inc.

"Bugs" (text only) is reprinted from THE FISH WITH THE DEEP SEA SMILE by Margaret Wise Brown by permission of Linnet Books, North Haven, CT. Copyright © 1966 Roberta Rauch.

"Yesterday's Paper" (text only) by Mabel Watts, reprinted with permission of the author.

"Ears Hear" (text only) from OODLES OF NOODLES, © 1964 by Lucia and James L. Hymes, Jr. Reprinted by permission of Addison-Wesley Publishing Company, Inc.

"Tommy" (text only) from BRONZEVILLE BOYS AND GIRLS by Gwendolyn Brooks, Copyright © 1956 by Gwendolyn Brooks Blakely. Selection reprinted by permission of HarperCollins Publishers.

Letter models in this program were used with permission of the publisher, Zaner-Bloser, Inc., Columbus, OH. From HANDWRITING: A WAY TO SELF EXPRESSION, copyright, 1993.

Product Development and Management: Leslie A. Baranowski

Photo Credits

Neal Farris: Cover

Diane J. Ali: 251, 265 top, 265 background, 297 panel 6 top right, 298 panel 2 background, 298 panel 5 center, 298 panel 5 bottom, 299 top left. Animals Animals/Breck P. Kent: 145 top, 145 bottom left, 297 panel 3 top right; Michael Fogden: 145 right; John Lemker: 265 bottom right; Raymond Mendez: 293 top left; Harold Taylor Abipp: 293 bottom right; Richard Kolar: 293 bottom

left; E.R. Degginger: 294 top right; J.H. Robinson: 294 top left; Earth Scenes–Donald Specker: 297 panel 6 center; Earth Scenes–E.R. Degginger: 298 panel 7. Cate Photography: 47, 68, 75, 167, 223 right, 223 left, 265 left. Kathy Ferguson: 297 panel 3 top right. Ken Karp: 11, 245 bottom right. Frances Roberts: 81 bottom right. H. Armstrong Roberts: 29, 245 top right, 245 center right, 245 bottom, 283

bottom left, 283 center left, 294 bottom left, 298 panel 4 top, 298 panel 4 top, 298 panel 2 bottom, 298 panel 5 top, 299 bottom left, 300 left. The Stock Market/David Wood: 65; Chuck Savage: 245 left; Lance Nelson: 257; A. & J. Verkaik: 265 center right; David Barnes: 283 top right; Zefa Hahn: 283 center right; Jose Pelaez: 283 bottom center; Frank Moscati: 283 center top; Connie Hansen: 298 panel 4 bottom. Tony Stone Images: 283 top left;

David Ball: 17; Fred Felleman: 255; Kevin Schaefer: 283 bottom right; James Balog: 293 top right; John Warden: 294 bottom right; David Young Wolff: 297 top left; Ross Harrison Koty: 297 top center left; Renee Lynn: 297 panel 6 bottom; Stephen Studd: 299 top right; Ralph Wetmore II: 300 right. Steve Vidler/Nawrocki Stock Photography: 81 top, 81 bottom left.

Illustrators

Dirk Wunderlich: Cover

Bernard Adnet: 39.
JoLynn Alcorn: 95, 104, 199.
Shirley Beckes: 85, 93, 149.
Nan Brooks: 303, 304.
Paige Billin-Frye: 189, 216, 230.
Ken Bowser: 297, 298.
Jenny Campbell: 92, 103, 116, 128, 160, 194, 208, 212, 218, 222.
Marilyn Cathcart: 249.
Eileen Elterman: 225.
Arthur Friedman: 289, 290.
Barbara Friedman: 53, 107, 115, 241.

Adam Gordon: 43, 293, 294.
Linda Graves: 49, 51.
Myron Grossman: 15, 54, 73, 203, 262.
Susan Hall: 127, 135, 139.
Laurie Hamilton: 35, 55, 117, 140.
John Stephen Henry: 170, 238.
Joan Holub: 74.
Linda Howard: 31.
Ann Iosa: 274.
Megan Jeffery: 157, 169, 185, 187, 210, 278.
Campbell Laird: 34.
Andy Levine: 163, 192, 176, 182, 211,

Jason Levinson: 83, 106, 118, 119, 141, 142, 161, 164, 173, 197.
Roseanne Litzinger: 301, 302.
Maria Pia Marrella: 223, 299, 300.
Patrick Merewether: 131.
Yoshi Miyake: 19.
John Nez: 291, 292.
Iva O'Connor: 57.
Olivia: 111, 275, 282.
Leah Palmer Preiss: 5.
Stacy Schuett: 269, 295, 296.
Sally Springer: 158, 172, 175, 181, 193,

242, 261, 280.

195, 196, 207, 209, 234, 248.
Matt Straub: 168.
Steve Sullivan: 6, 14, 84, 148, 226, 250, 270.
Don Tate: 94, 105, 129, 217, 243, 272.
George Ulrich: 12, 147.
Anna Veltfort: 13.
Susan Williams: 256
Michael Woo: 220, 279.

Functional art:
Diane Ali, Batelman Illustration, Moffit Cecil, Adam Gordon, Larry Lee, John Quinn, Sintora Regina Vanderhorst

CONTENTS

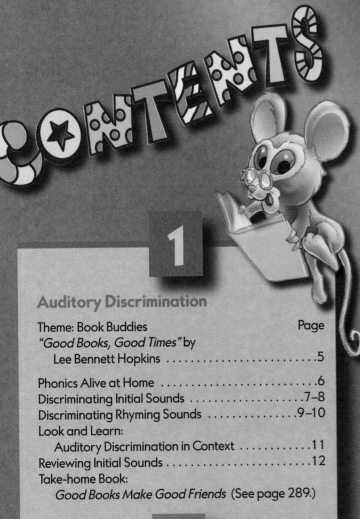

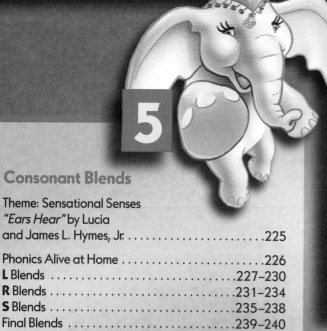

GOOD BOOKS, GOOD TIMES!

Good books.
Good times.
Good stories.
Good rhymes.

Good beginnings.
Good ends.
Good people.
Good friends.

Good fiction.
Good facts.
Good adventures.
Good acts.

Good stories.
Good rhymes.
Good books.
Good times.

Lee Bennett Hopkins

Critical Thinking

Why do you like some books more than others?
Where is the best place to read a book?

LESSON 1: Introduction to Auditory Discrimination

Dear Family,

In this unit, your child will be listening for words that begin with the same sound and also for words that rhyme. He or she will be talking about the fun of reading good books. You can enjoy this unit with your child by trying these activities at home.

● Read the poem "Good Books, Good Times!" on the reverse side of this page as your child follows along.

● Talk about a favorite book you have read together.

● Ask your child to listen as you read the poem aloud again. Name pairs of rhyming words together (**times/rhymes, ends/friends, facts/acts**).

● Visit your local library and find a new book to share.

Apreciada Familia:

En esta unidad se enseñarán las palabras que empiezan con el mismo sonido y palabras que riman. Los niños estarán hablando de lo divertido que es leer buenos libros. Ustedes pueden disfrutar junto al niño de esta unidad haciendo esta actividad juntos en la casa.

● Lean, en voz alta, el poema en la página 5 mientras su hijo lo repite.

● Hablen del libro que leyeron juntos y que les gustó.

● Pidan al niño que escuche el poema mientras se le lee en voz alta otra vez. Nombren pares de palabras que rimen (**times/rhymes, ends/friends, facts/acts**).

● Visiten la biblioteca del vecindario y busquen un libro que puedan compartir.

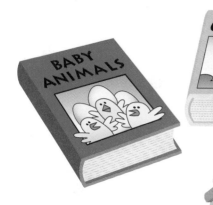

PROJECT

Have fun with beginning sounds. Say a word like **book** and encourage your child to say another word, such as **bike**, that begins with the same sound. Take turns thinking of words.

PROYECTO

Diviértanse con los sonidos. Diga una palabra, por ejemplo **book** y anime al niño a decir otra que empiece con el mismo sonido, tal como, **bike**. Túrnense para pensar en las palabras.

Name the first picture in each row. Then circle and color the pictures in the row whose names begin with the same sound.

LESSON 2: Discriminating Initial Sounds

7

Say the names of the pictures on each book. If their names begin with the same sound, circle the book.

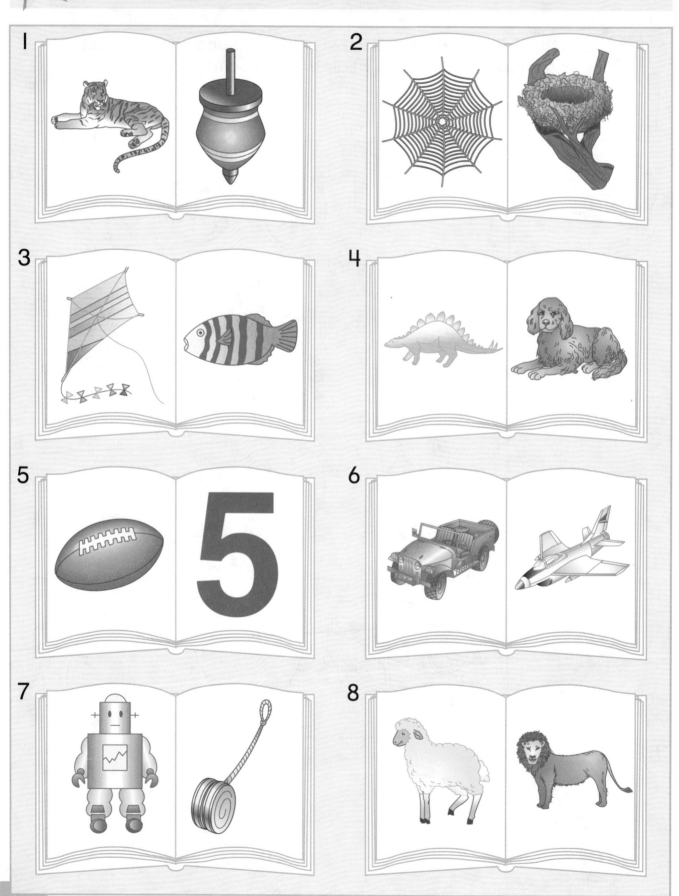

LESSON 2: Discriminating Initial Sounds

Name the first picture in each row. Then circle the pictures whose names rhyme.

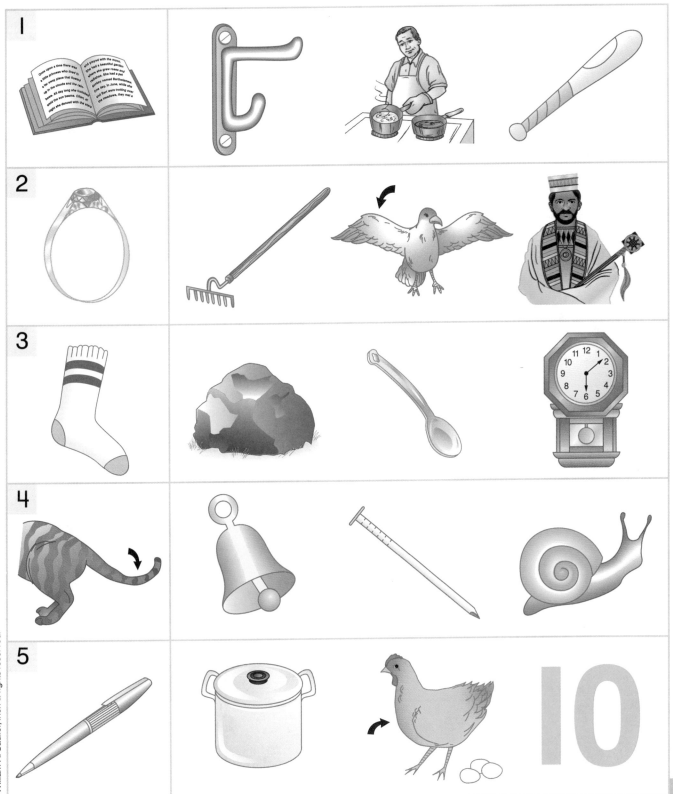

LESSON 3: Discriminating Rhyming Sounds

9

Say the name of each picture. Draw lines to connect the pictures whose names rhyme.

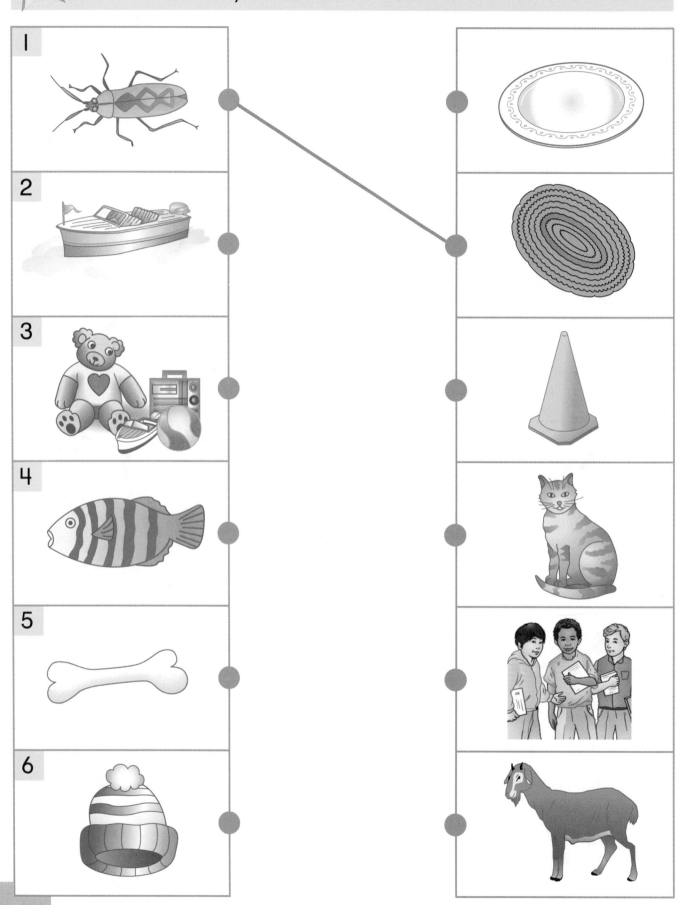

LESSON 3: Discriminating Rhyming Sounds

Look and Learn

Look at the pictures.
Then read and talk about them.

Look at a good book.
Books are stories written down.
Some books tell made-up stories.
Some books tell true stories.
It's fun to read books, and
it's fun to write them, too.

What would you like to
write a book about?

RAIN FOREST

LESSON 4: Auditory
Discrimination in Context

11

The book covers on each shelf have pictures whose names begin with the same sound. Help Dan and Jen find the books that belong on each shelf and write the numbers there.

PARADES

I like to see parades
with the marching bands
and big bass drums;
They make me want to dance
and clap my hands.

People ride in convertible cars
and smile and wave at you
and clowns come down the street
and make you laugh.

A parade makes everybody happy;
people talk and dance and sing—
I like to watch parades
more than any other thing.

Karama Fufuka

Critical Thinking

Why do people have parades?
What other kinds of celebrations are fun?

LESSON 5: Introduction to Consonant Sounds

Dear Family,

In this unit about celebrations, your child will learn the sounds of the consonant letters. As your child progresses through this unit, you may wish to try these activities together at home.

● Read the poem "Parades" on the reverse side of this page.

● Then talk about parades. Have you ever seen a parade together? Have you or your child ever been in a parade?

Apreciada Familia:

Esta unidad es sobre las celebraciones. Los niños aprenderán el sonido de las consonantes. A medida que se avanza en la unidad, pueden hacer estas actividades con su hijo.

● Lea el poema "Parades" en la página 13.

● Luego hablen sobre los desfiles. ¿Han asistido a algún desfile juntos? ¿Ha participado alguno de ustedes en un desfile?

● The consonant letters of the alphabet are shown above. Help your child find some of these consonants in the poem.

● What consonants are in your names? Can you find words with those same consonant sounds in the poem?

● Las consonantes son mostradas arriba. Ayude al niño a encontrar algunas consonantes en el poema.

● ¿Cuántas consonantes hay en su nombre? ¿Puede encontrar palabras con esas consonantes en el poema?

PROJECT

What kinds of celebrations are special for your family? Look at a calendar together and mark the dates of a few of them. Talk about why these days are important. How does your family celebrate them? Help your child find and name some consonants in the names of these celebrations.

PROYECTO

¿Cuáles celebraciones son especiales en su familia? Juntos busquen en un calendario las fechas de algunas. Hablen sobre esos días importantes. ¿Cómo celebra la familia esos días? Ayude al niño a encontrar algunas consonantes en los nombres de esas celebraciones.

The letters **Ff, Mm, Ss, Tt, Hh, Bb,** are partner letters. Color the clowns' hats with matching partner letters the same color.

Look at the first letter in each word. Circle the words in each row that begin with the same consonant.

1

(Fred)   (fun)   Tom   (fox)

2

bed   peach   beach   Bess

3

Ron   Hank   hill   hit

4

son   cat   Sue   Sam

5

Mike   moon   nose   map

6

Tim   tie   toad   Ed

LESSON 6: Letter Recognition: **Ff, Mm, Ss, Tt, Hh, Bb**

F f

⭐ **F**an starts with the sound of **f**. Circle and color the pictures whose names begin with the sound of **f**.

1	2	3	4
5	6	7	8
		9	10
		11	12

LESSON 7: Recognizing the Sound of Initial Consonant **f**

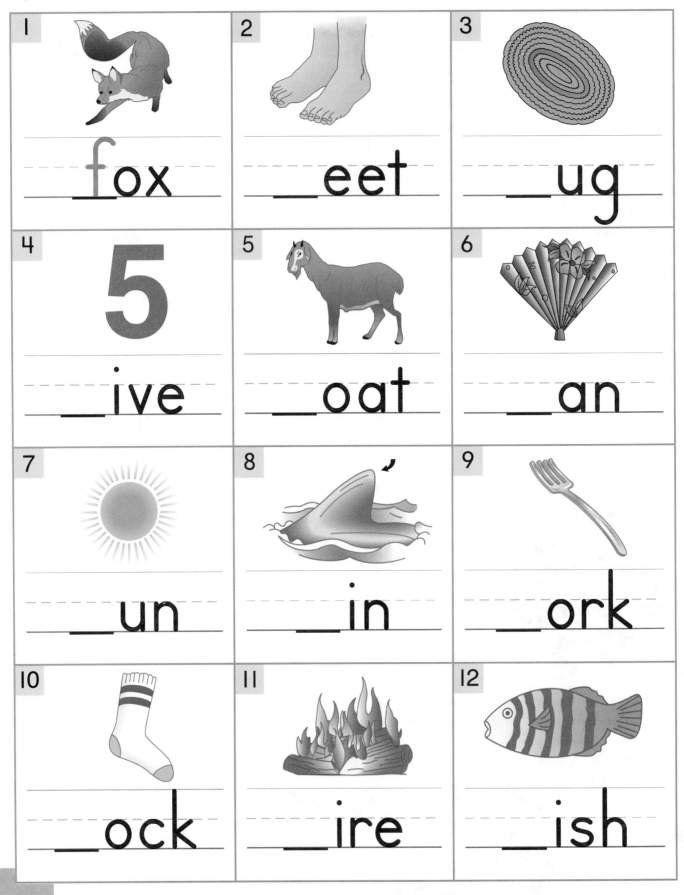

1 **f**ox	2 __eet	3 __ug
4 __ive	5 __oat	6 __an
7 __un	8 __in	9 __ork
10 __ock	11 __ire	12 __ish

LESSON 7: Recognizing and Writing Initial Consonant **f**

Mask starts with the sound of **m**. Circle and color the pictures whose names begin with the sound of **m**.

Mm

1

2

3

4

5

6

7

8

9

10

11

12

LESSON 8: Recognizing the Sound of Initial Consonant **m**

19

1 m an	2 __an	3 __eat
4 __ail	5 __oon	6 __op
7 __ebra	8 __ap	9 __ule
10 __ask	11 __ut	12 __ilk

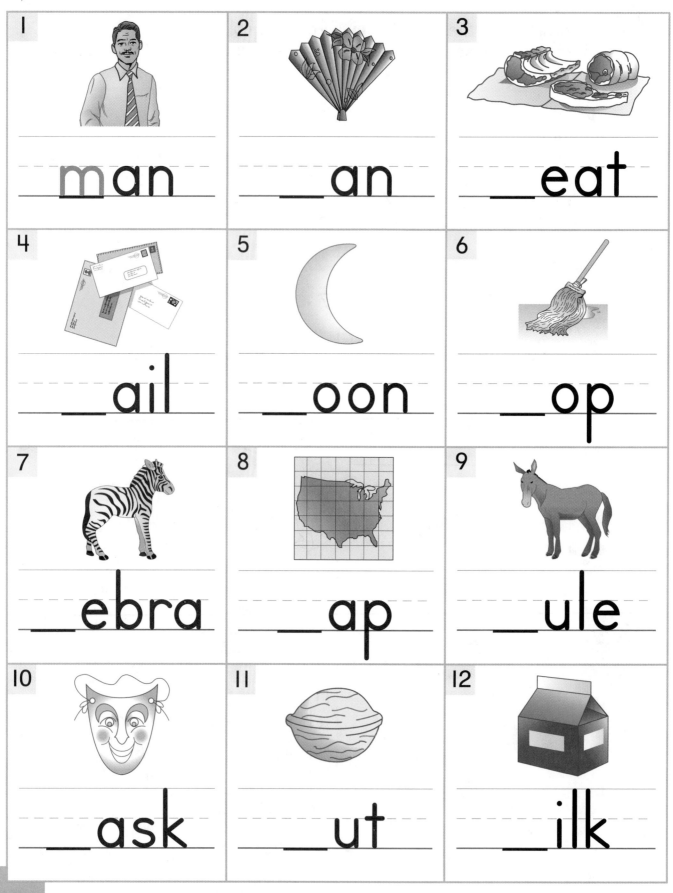

Seal starts with the sound of **s**. Cross out the pictures whose names do not begin with the sound of **s**.

Ss

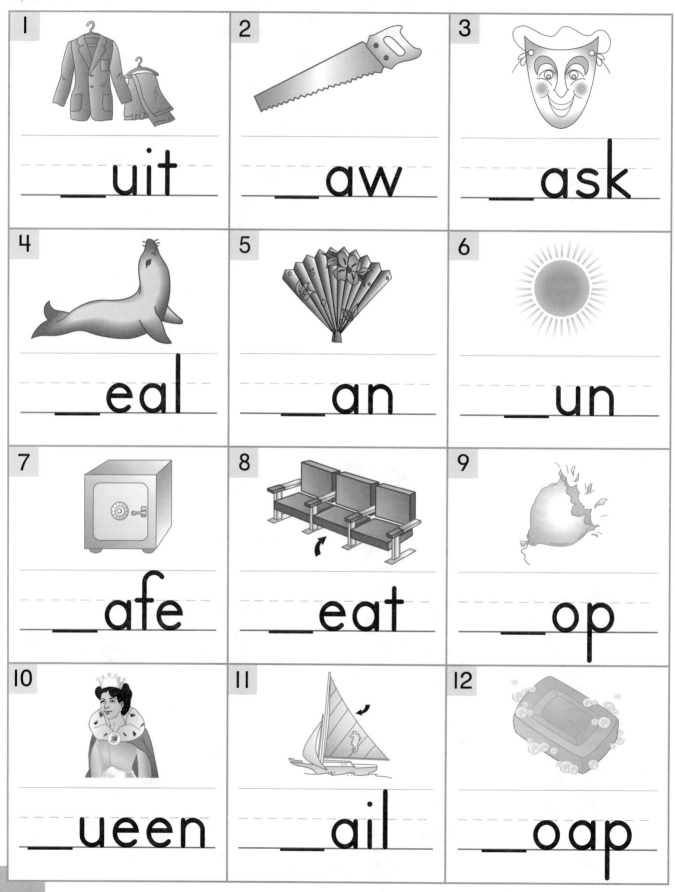

1 ___uit	2 ___aw	3 ___ask
4 ___eal	5 ___an	6 ___un
7 ___afe	8 ___eat	9 ___op
10 ___ueen	11 ___ail	12 ___oap

Circle the pictures in each row whose ending sound is the same as the sound of the letter in the box.

1	leaf	hat	calf	**f**
2	sun	ham	drum	**m**
3	house	cap	glass	**s**
4	giraffe	scarf	scissors	**f**
5	sock	team	gym	**m**
6	bus	goose	horn	**s**

LESSON 10: Identifying Final Consonants **f, m, s**

Print the missing letter on the line under each picture.

1	2	3
___ap	___an	___un

4	5	6
___en	___ix	___ix

7	8	9
___in	___aw	___ox

10	11	12
bu___	dru___	lea___

Toys starts with the sound of **t**. Circle and color the pictures whose names begin with the sound of **t**.

T t

LESSON 11: Recognizing the Sound of Initial Consonant **t**

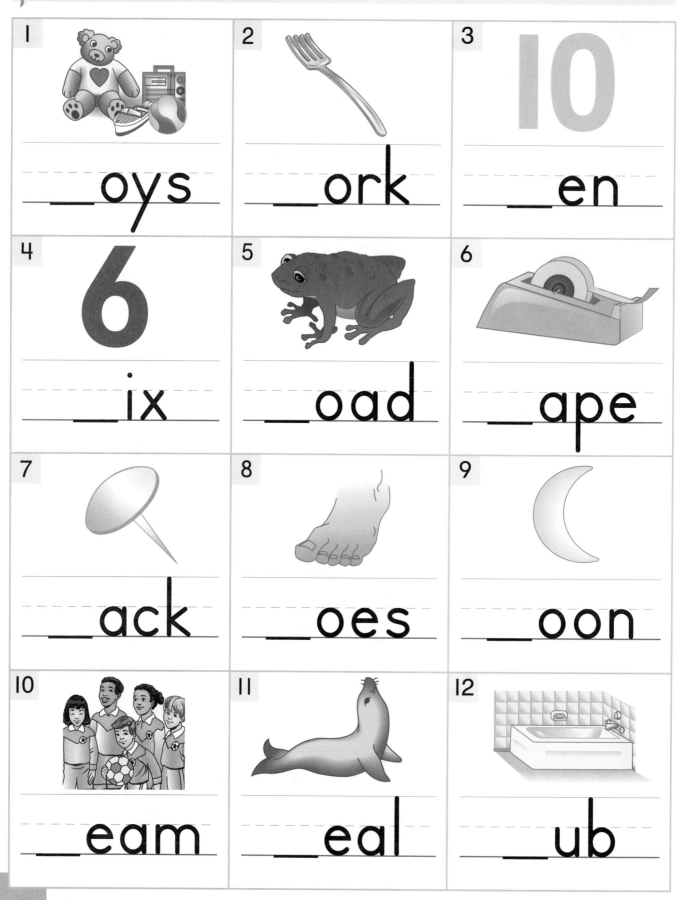

1. __oys

2. __ork

3. __en

4. __ix

5. __oad

6. __ape

7. __ack

8. __oes

9. __oon

10. __eam

11. __eal

12. __ub

Horn starts with the sound of **h**. Circle and color the pictures whose names begin with the sound of **h**.

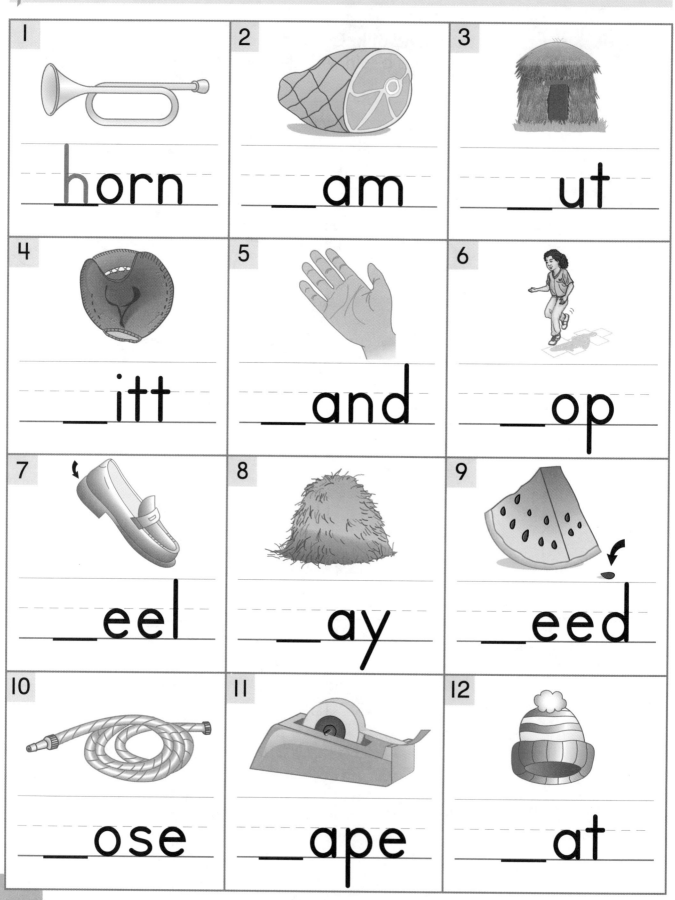

1. horn

2. __am

3. __ut

4. __itt

5. __and

6. __op

7. __eel

8. __ay

9. __eed

10. __ose

11. __ape

12. __at

LESSON 12: Recognizing and Writing Initial Consonant **h**

Balloon starts with the sound of **b**. Circle and color the pictures whose names begin with the sound of **b**.

Bb

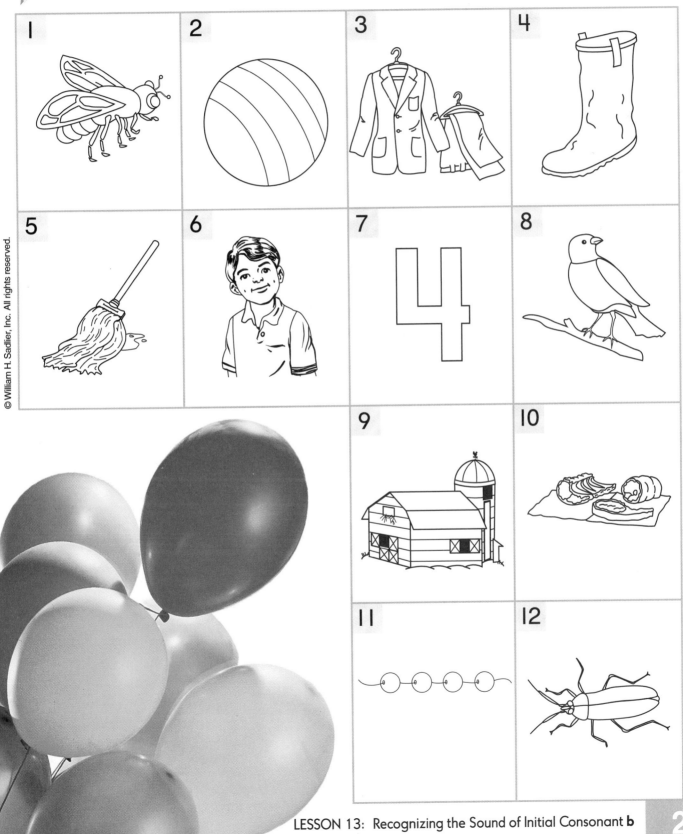

1	2	3	4
5	6	7	8
		9	10
		11	12

LESSON 13: Recognizing the Sound of Initial Consonant **b**

29

Print **b** on the line under each picture whose name begins with the sound of **b**.

1 ___and	2 ___an	3 ___ib
4 ___un	5 ___ed	6 ___ug
7 ___ox	8 ___en	9 ___at
10 ___ag	11 ___oy	12 ___ug

Color the pictures whose ending sound is the same as the sound of the letter on the flag.

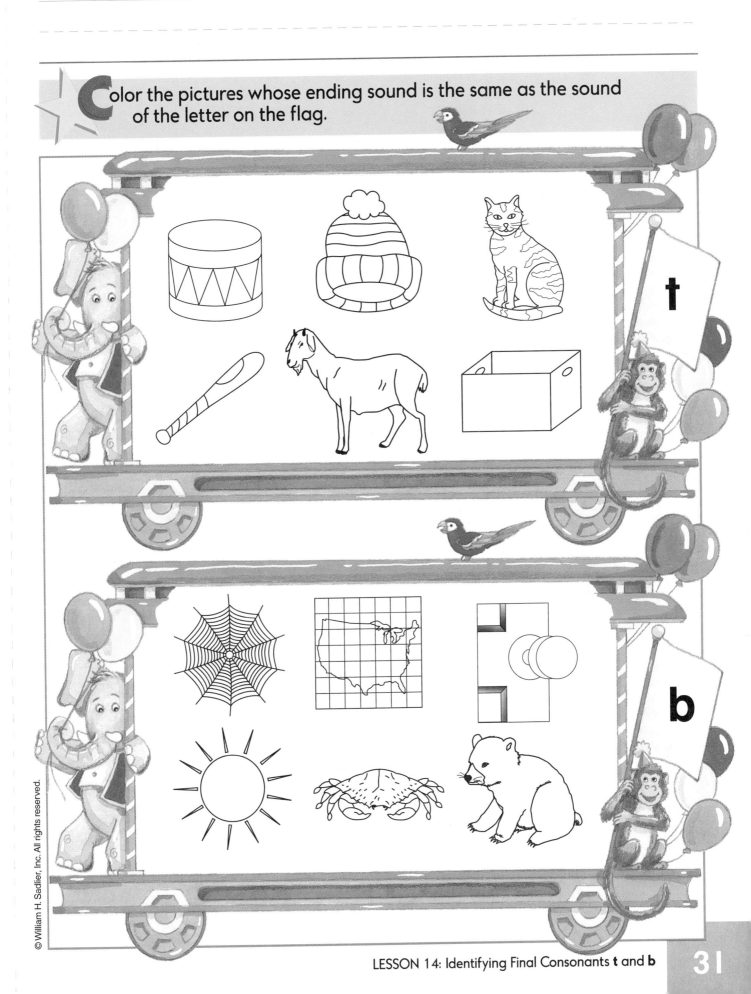

LESSON 14: Identifying Final Consonants **t** and **b**

31

In each game, score a tic-tac-toe by drawing a line through the three pictures whose names begin with the same sound.

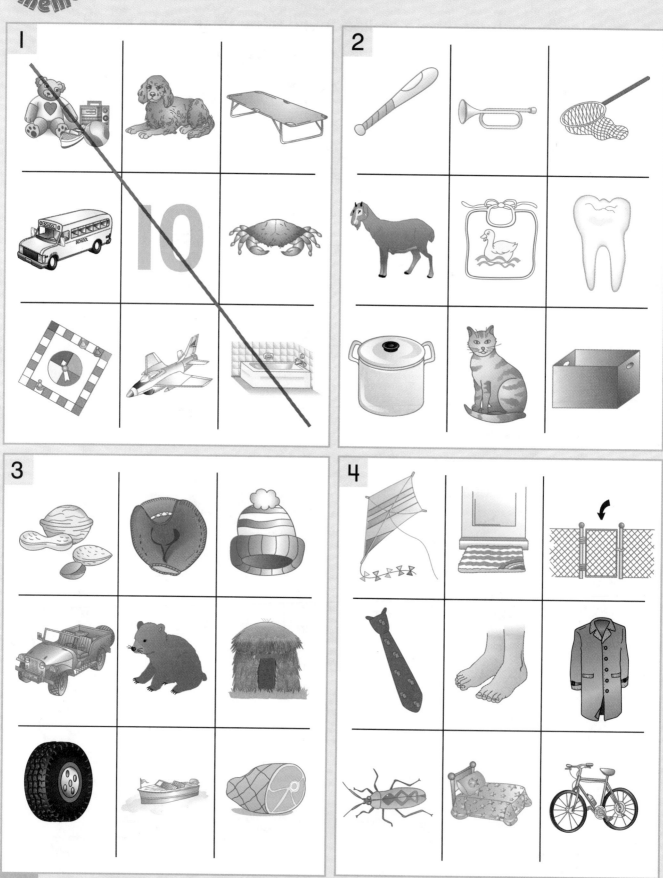

Circle the pictures whose beginning sound is the same as the sound of the letter in the box.

1 **f**			
2 **m**			
3 **s**			
4 **t**			
5 **h**			
6 **b**			

Check-Up Cut out the letters at the bottom of the page. Then say the name of the picture on each flag. Glue the letter that stands for the beginning sound of the picture name on the flag.

f   m   s   t   h   b

LESSON 15: Assessing Consonants **f, m, s, t, h, b**

The letters **Ll, Dd, Cc, Nn, Gg** and **Ww** are partner letters. Find partner letters on the cars. Color the cars with partner letters the same color.

1			
Ll	like	Len	~~ice~~

2			
Dd	Dee	box	dance

3			
Cc	owl	cars	Cal

4			
Nn	Nell	mask	nest

5			
Gg	goat	Gail	pup

6			
Ww	Walt	van	wave

LESSON 16: Letter Recognition: **Ll, Dd, Cc, Nn, Gg, Ww**

L l

Leaf starts with the sound of **l**. Circle and color the pictures whose names begin with the sound of **l**.

1 · 2 · 3 · 4

5 · 6 · 7 · 8

9 · 10 · 11 · 12

13 · 14 · 15 · 16

LESSON 17: Recognizing the Sound of Initial Consonant **l**

37

1	2	3
__eg	__amb	__ask

4	5	6
eggs bread milk juice apples		
__oys	__ist	__ime

7	8	9
		5
__eash	__eaf	__ive

10	11	12
_____		
__ine	__un	__ake

Duck starts with the sound of **d**. Circle and color the pictures whose names begin with the sound of **d**.

Dd

Print **d** on the line under each picture whose name begins with the sound of **d**.

1 __uck	2 __ug	3 __eer
4 __oor	5 __op	6 __ig
7 __ug	8 __ish	9 __og
10 __ive	11 __ire	12 __oll

LESSON 18: Recognizing and Writing Initial Consonant **d**

Cake starts with the sound of **c**. Cross out the picture in each row whose name does not begin with the sound of **c**.

Cc

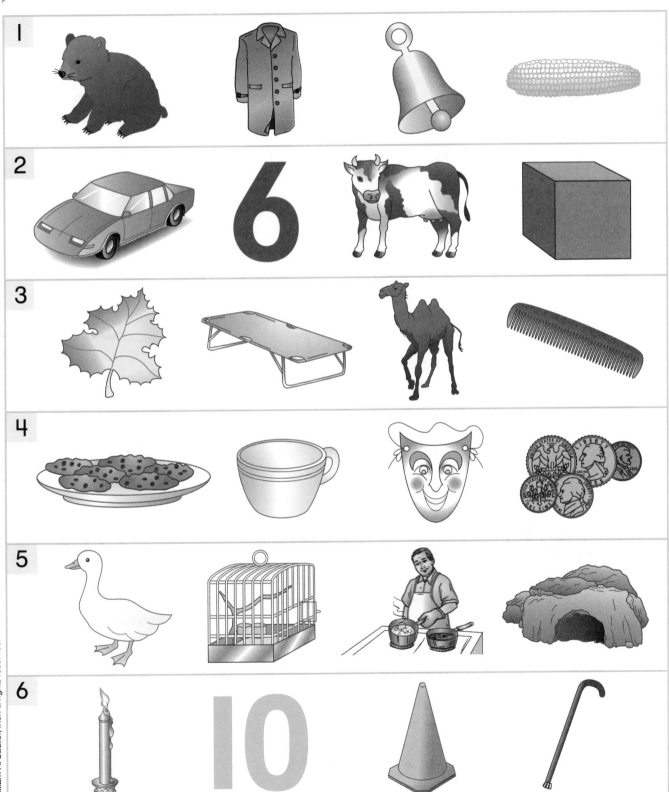

1
2
3
4
5
6

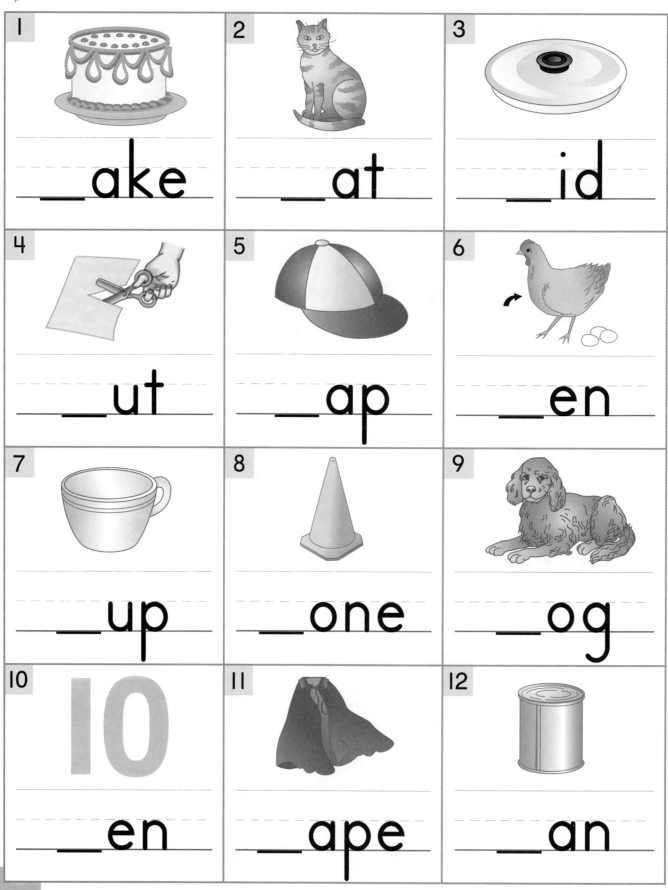

1 __ake	2 __at	3 __id
4 __ut	5 __ap	6 __en
7 __up	8 __one	9 __og
10 __en	11 __ape	12 __an

Circle and color the pictures in each box whose ending sound is the same as the sound of the letter on the sail.

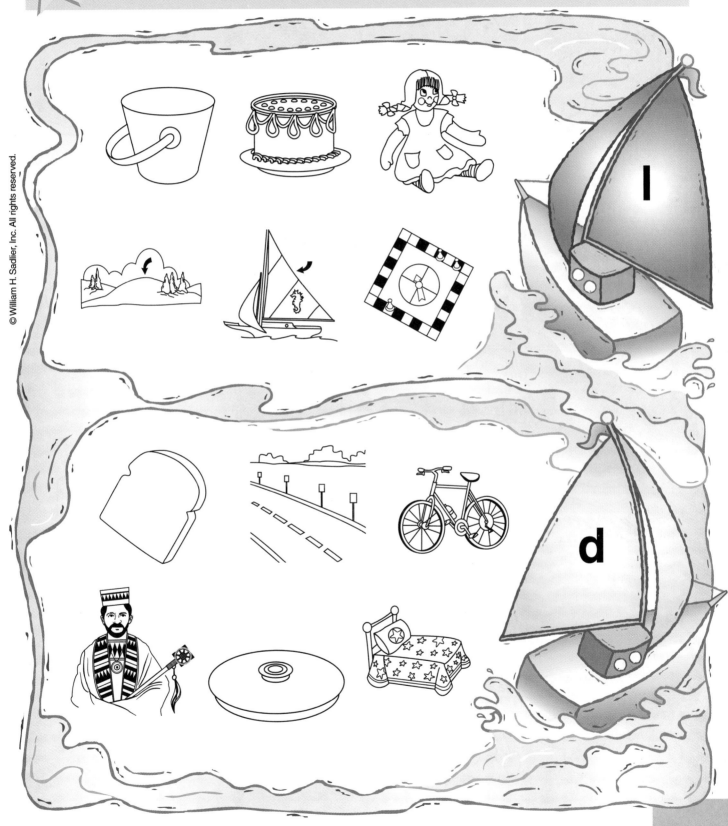

Use ▭▭▭▭ to color the pictures whose names start with **l**.
Use ▭▭▭▭ to color the pictures whose names start with **d**.
Use ▭▭▭▭ to color the pictures whose names start with **c**.

N n

Nest starts with the sound of **n**. Circle and color the pictures whose names begin with the sound of **n**.

Print **n** on the line under each picture whose name begins with the sound of **n**.

1 __et	2 __eed	3 __uts
4 __ail	5 __ap	6 __eam
7 __urse	8 __ar	9 __est
10 __ote	11 __og	12 __ose

Gift starts with the sound of **g**. Circle and color the pictures whose names begin with the sound of **g**.

Gg

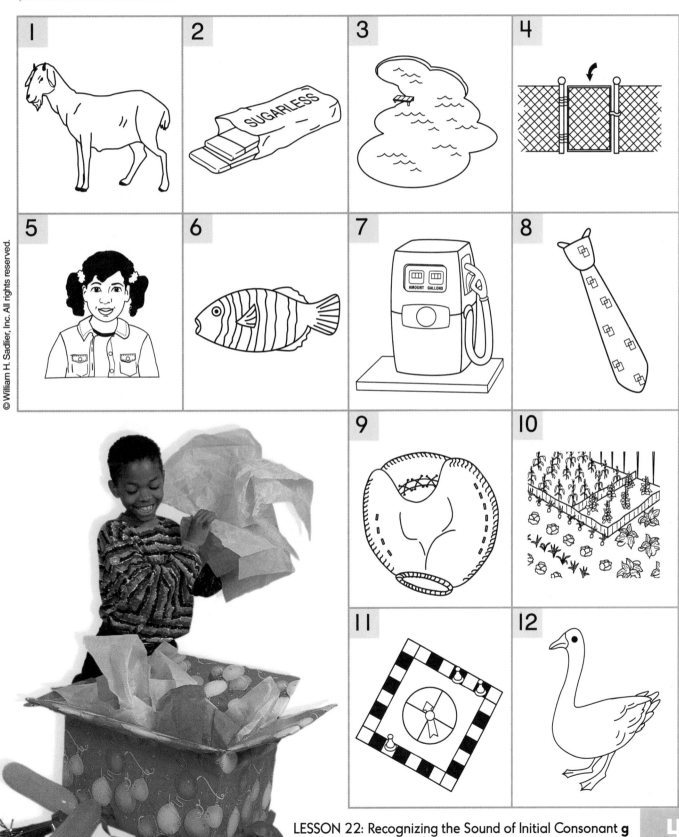

1
2
3
4
5
6
7
8
9
10
11
12

LESSON 22: Recognizing the Sound of Initial Consonant **g**

47

Print **g** on the line under each picture whose name begins with the sound of **g**.

1 __ift

2 __ane

3 __as

4 __esk

5 __um

6 __ail

7 __eat

8 __ate

9 __irl

10 __oat

11 __ame

12 __ock

Wagon starts with the sound of **w**. Circle and color the pictures whose names begin with the sound of **w**.

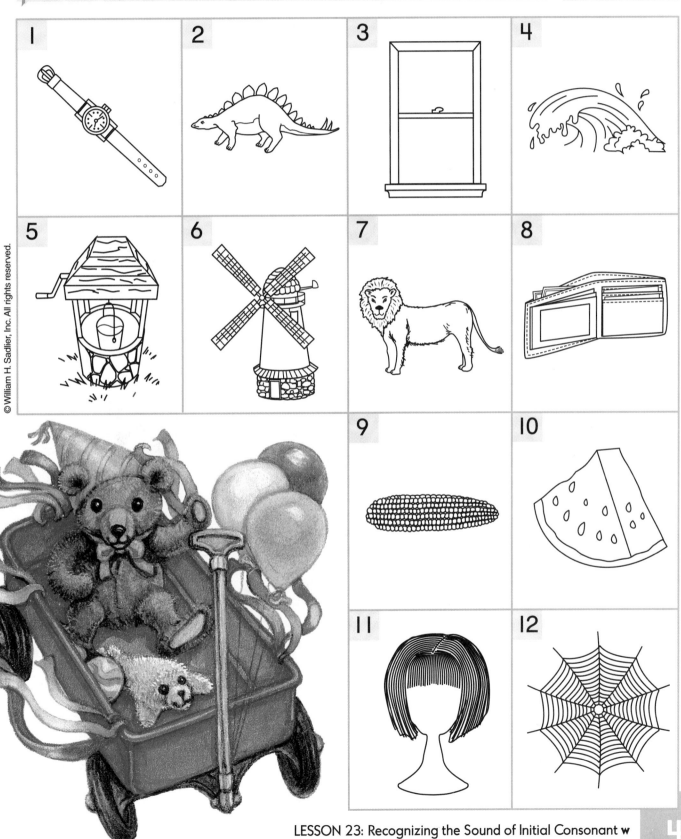

1

2

3

4

5

6

7

8

9

10

11

12

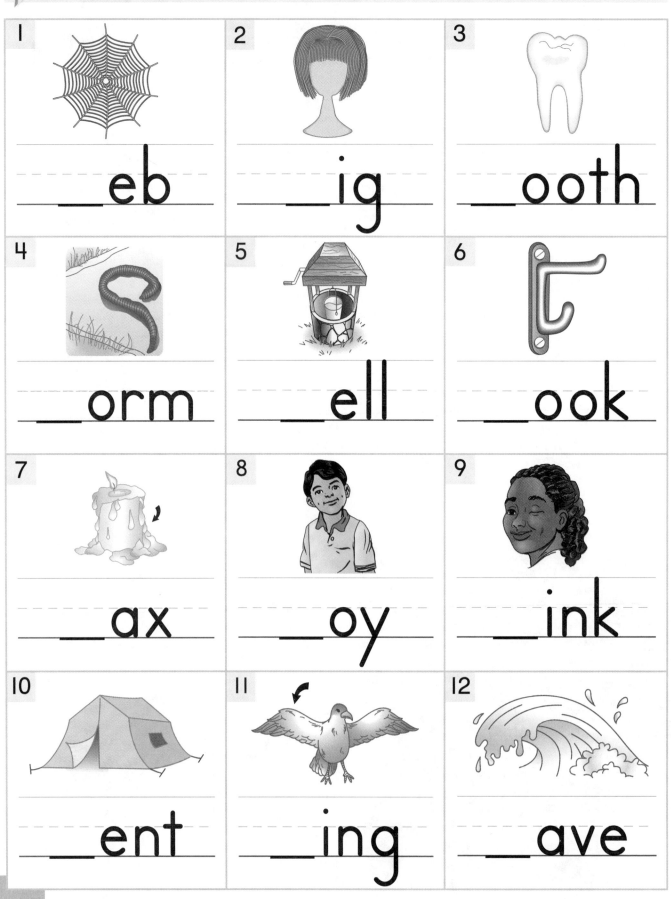

1 __eb	2 __ig	3 __ooth
4 __orm	5 __ell	6 __ook
7 __ax	8 __oy	9 __ink
10 __ent	11 __ing	12 __ave

Circle and color the pictures whose ending sound is the same as the sound of the letter on the boy's vest.

Print the missing letter on the line under each picture.

1 __est

2 __irl

3 __eb

4 __ink

5 __ate

6 __uts

7 __as

8 __ell

9 __ose

10 he__

11 fla__

12 su__

Say the name of each picture. Choose the letter that stands for its beginning sound. Print the letter on the line.

l d c n g w

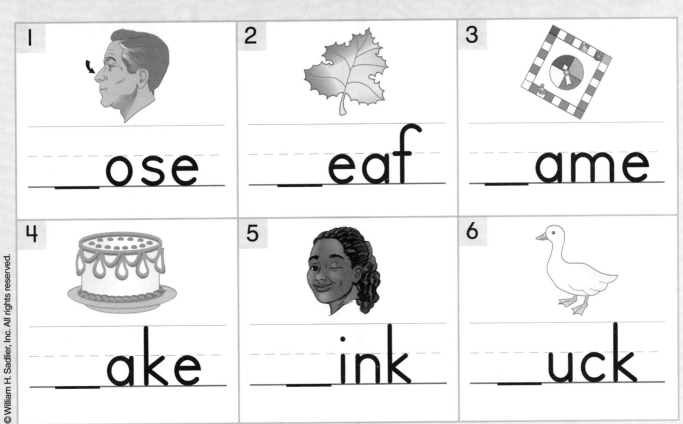

1 __ose	2 __eaf	3 __ame
4 __ake	5 __ink	6 __uck

Cut out the pictures at the bottom of the page. Glue each picture on the party invitation under the letter that stands for the beginning sound of the picture name.

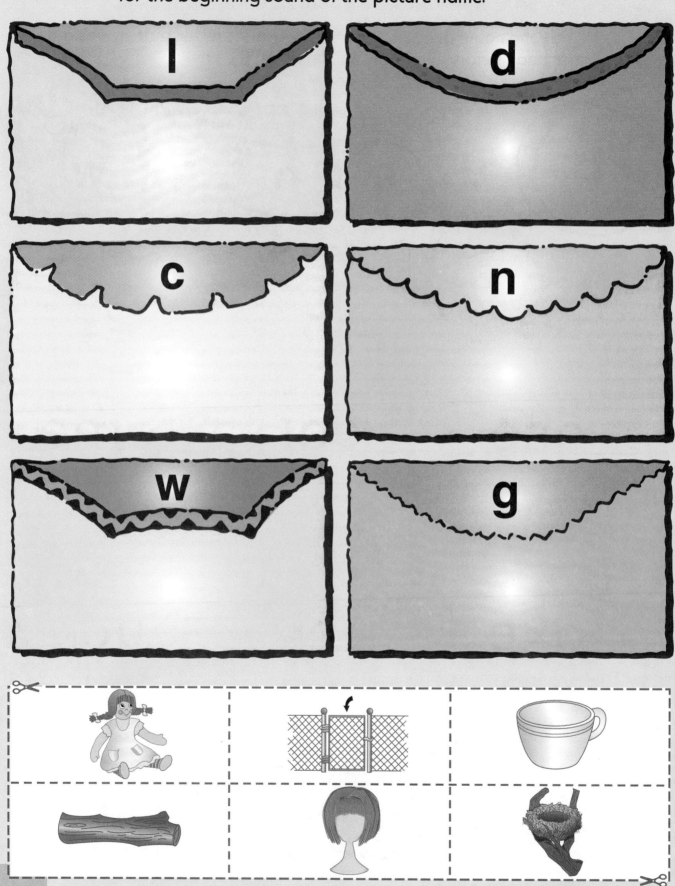

LESSON 25: Assessing Consonants **l, d, c, n, g, w**

The letters **Pp, Rr, Kk, Jj, Qq,** and **Vv** are partner letters. Find partner letters on the kites. Color the kites with partner letters the same color.

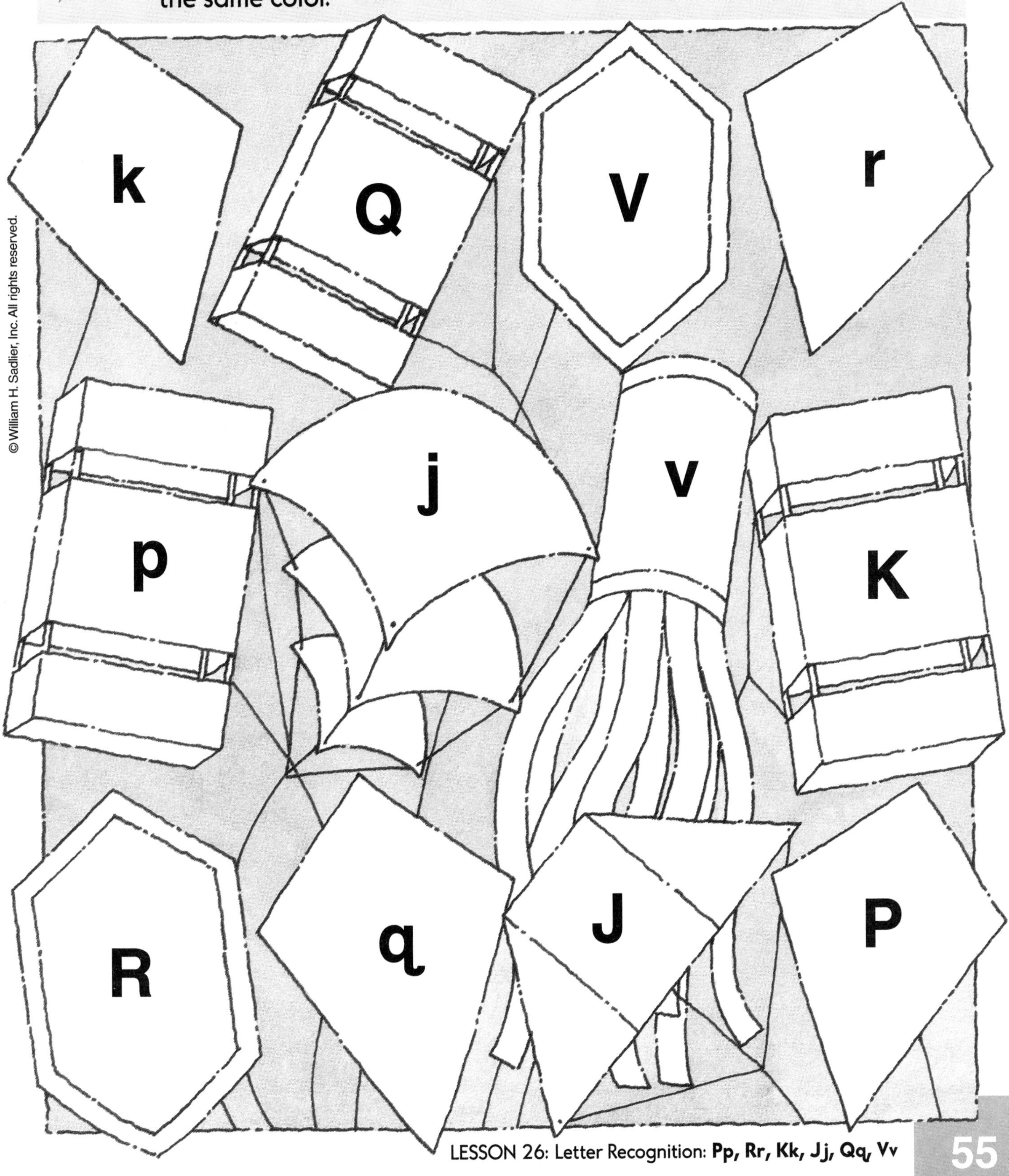

k

Q

V

r

p

j

v

K

R

q

J

P

Look at the partner letters in the box. Cross out the word in each row that does not begin with one of the partner letters in the box.

1	**Pp**	Pete	parade	gift
2	**Rr**	noisy	Rosita	red
3	**Kk**	kitten	hammer	Kate
4	**Jj**	ink	Jim	jacket
5	**Qq**	garden	quarter	Quinn
6	**Vv**	Val	wall	van

Pig starts with the sound of **p**. Circle and color the pictures whose names begin with the sound of **p**.

Pp

1	2	3	4

5	6	7	8

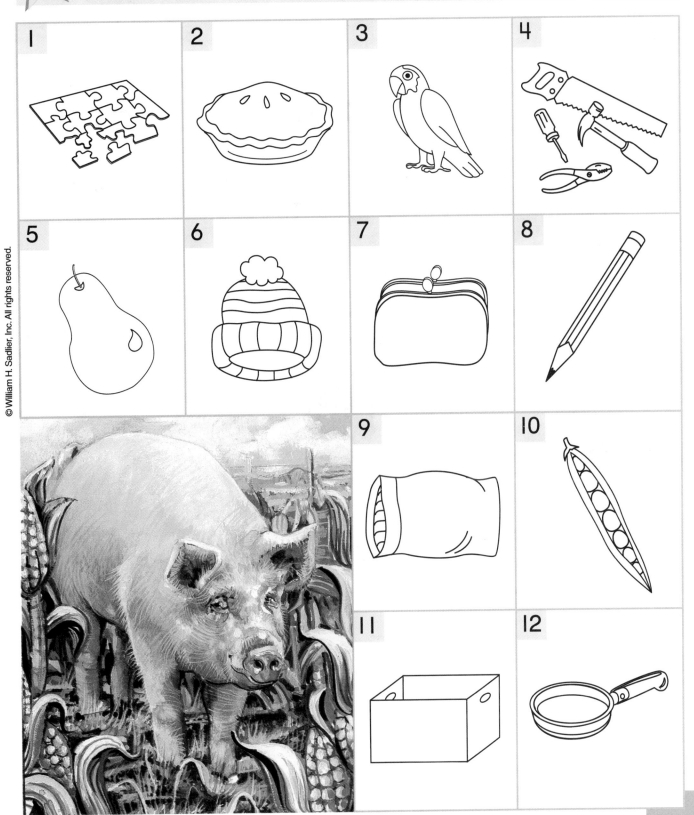

9	10

11	12

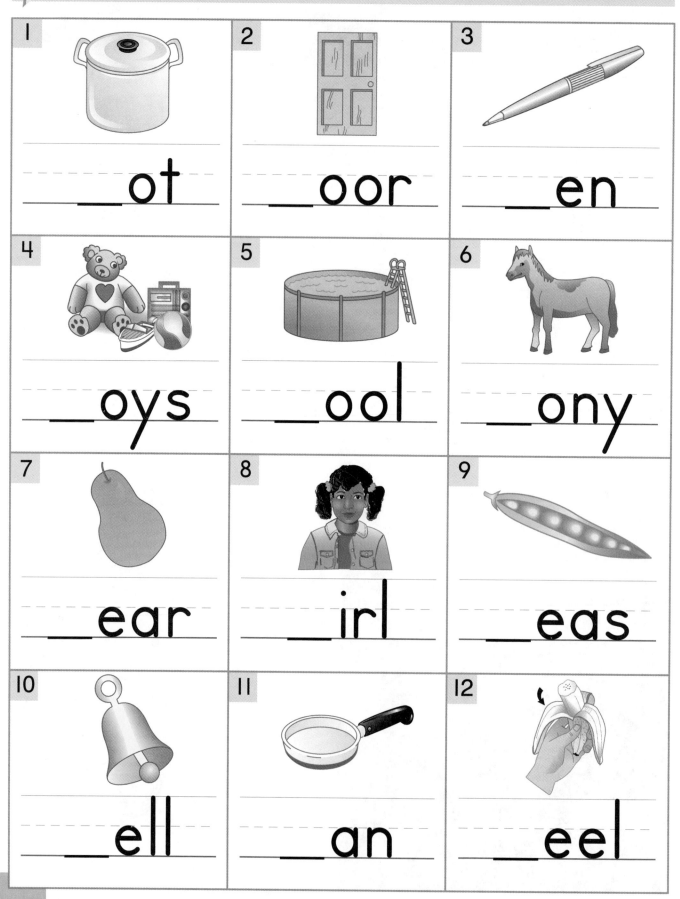

1 ___ot

2 ___oor

3 ___en

4 ___oys

5 ___ool

6 ___ony

7 ___ear

8 ___irl

9 ___eas

10 ___ell

11 ___an

12 ___eel

LESSON 27: Recognizing and Writing Initial Consonant **p**

Ride starts with the sound of **r**. Circle and color the pictures whose names begin with the sound of **r**.

Rr

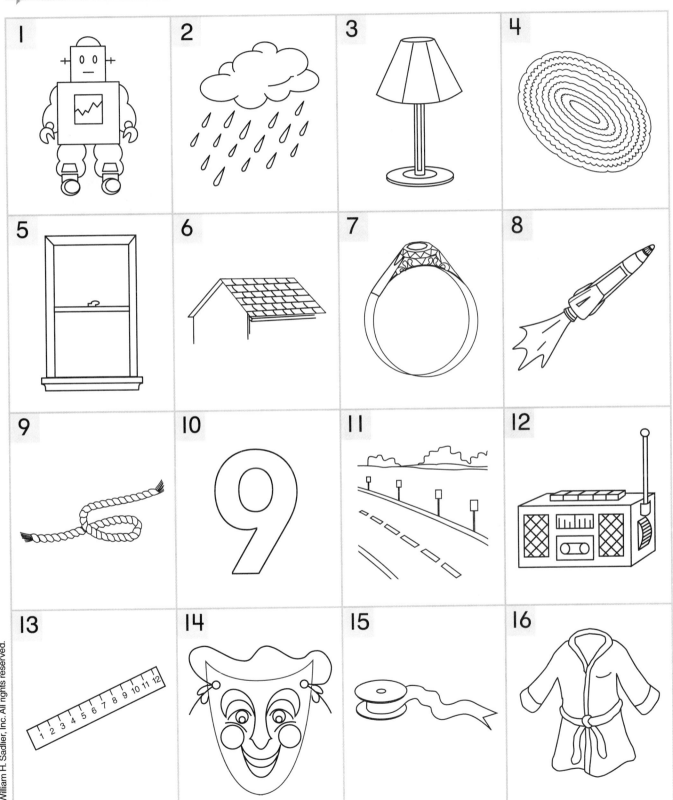

LESSON 28: Recognizing the Sound of Initial Consonant **r**

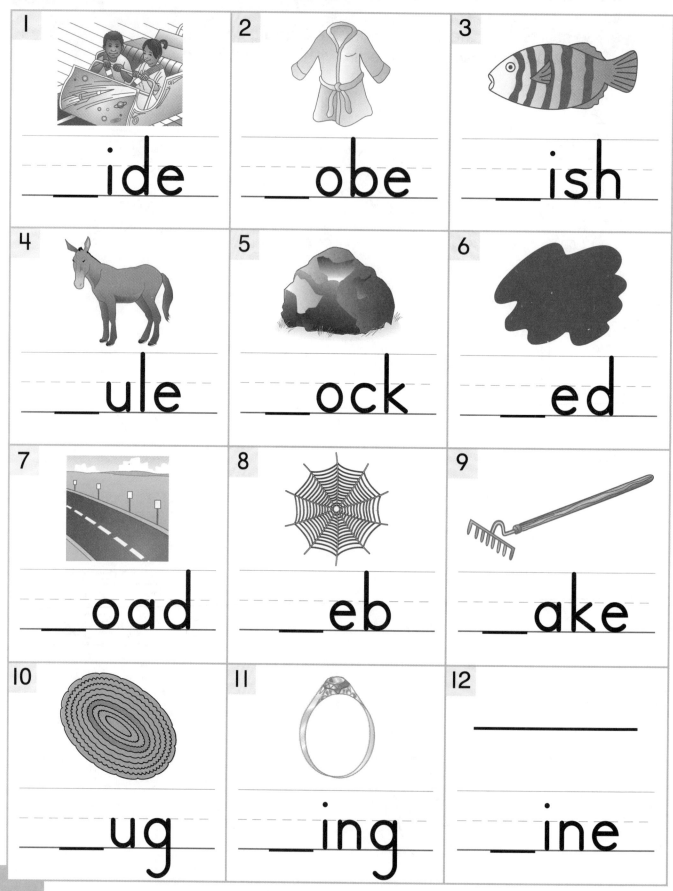

1. __ide

2. __obe

3. __ish

4. __ule

5. __ock

6. __ed

7. __oad

8. __eb

9. __ake

10. __ug

11. __ing

12. __ine

Kk

King starts with the sound of **k**. Circle the pictures in each row whose names begin with the sound of **k**.

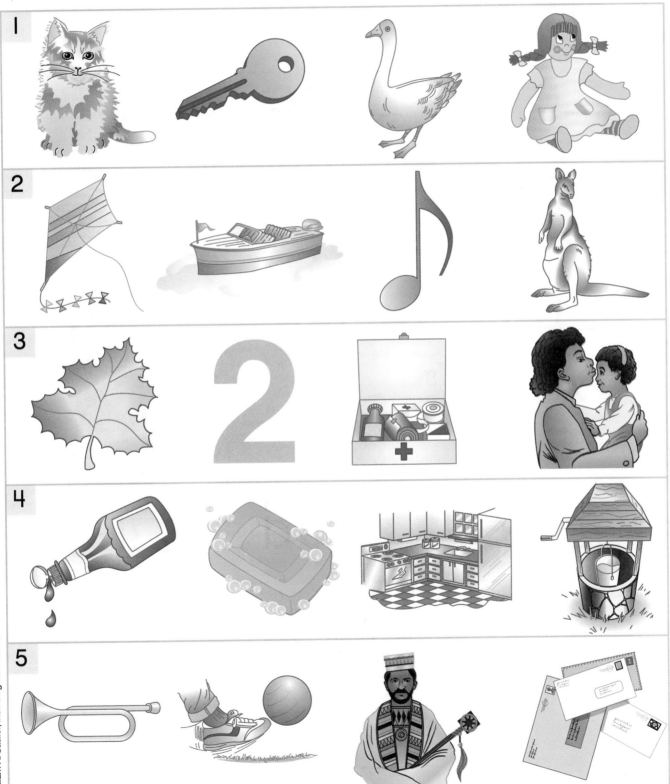

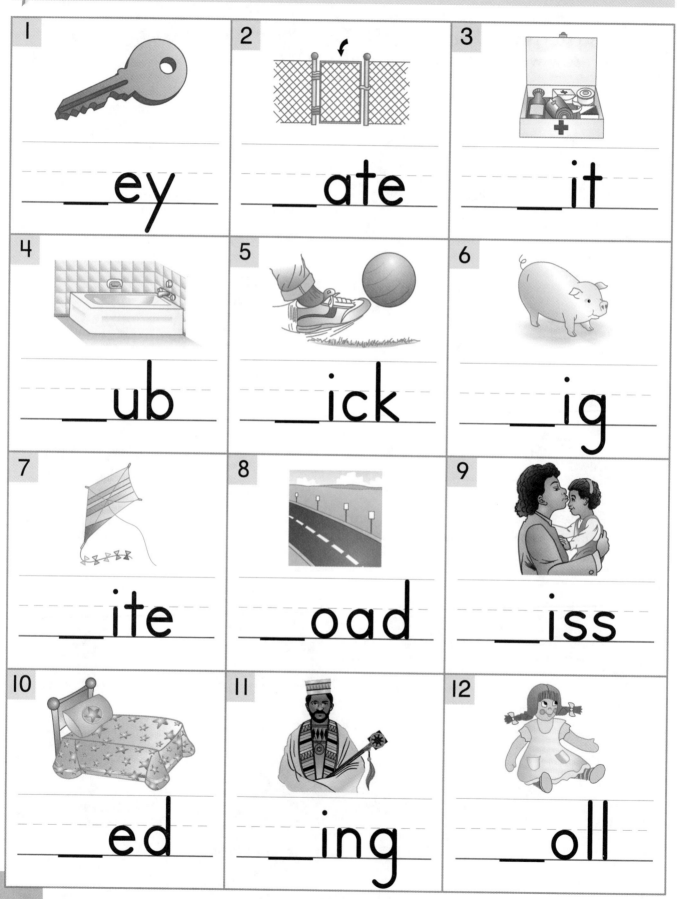

1 ___ey

2 ___ate

3 ___it

4 ___ub

5 ___ick

6 ___ig

7 ___ite

8 ___oad

9 ___iss

10 ___ed

11 ___ing

12 ___oll

Circle and color the pictures whose ending sound is the same as the sound of the letter in the box.

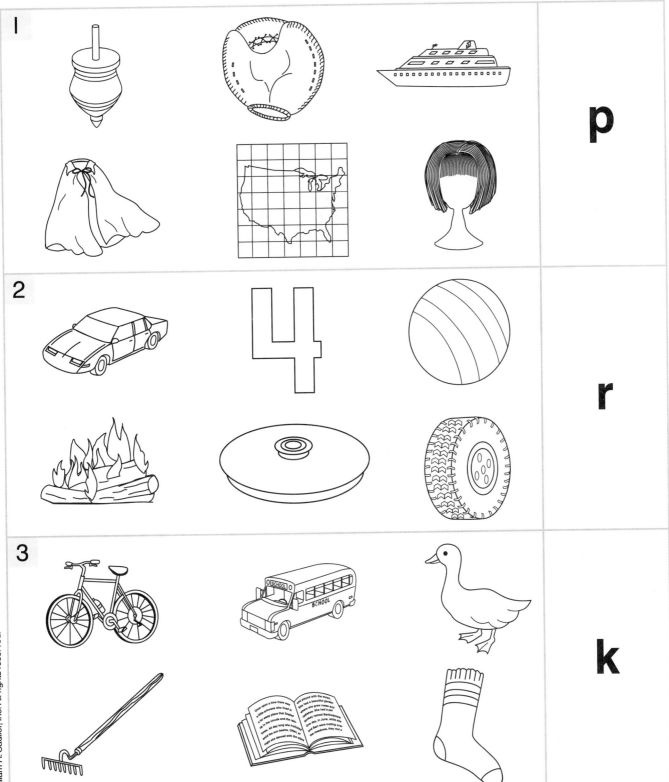

1   **p**

2   **r**

3   **k**

LESSON 30: Identifying Final Consonants **p, r, k**

63

Print the letter that stands for the missing sound on the line under each picture.

1	2	3
__ite	__ock	__ig

4	5	6
__ug	__ing	__an

7	8	9
sta__	boo__	ma__

10	11	12
hoo__	cu__	ja__

Juggle starts with the sound of **j**. Circle and color the pictures whose names begin with the sound of **j**.

Jj

1

2

3

4

5

6

7

8

9

10

11

12

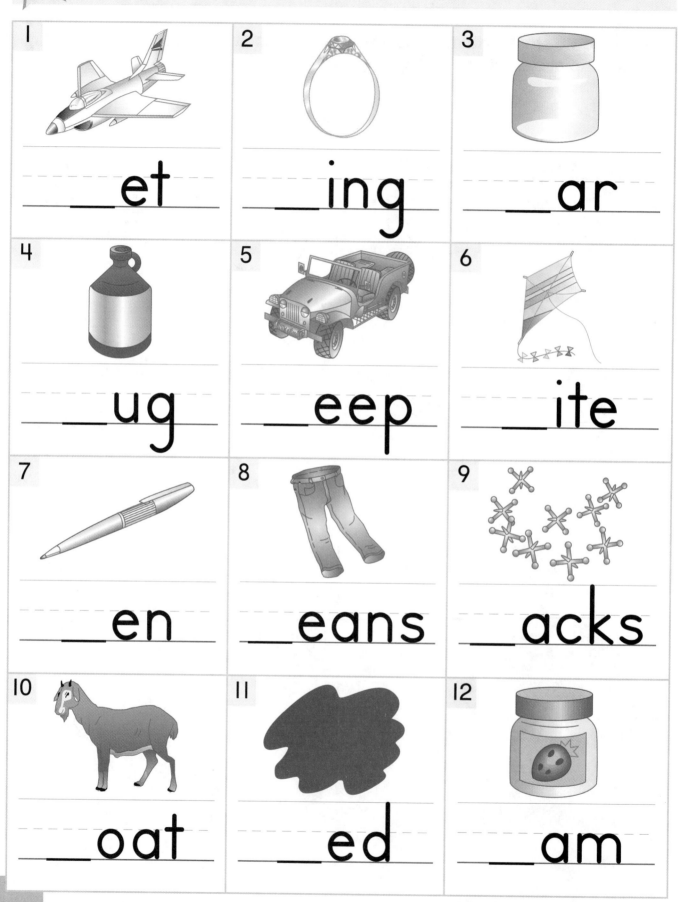

1 ____et

2 ____ing

3 ____ar

4 ____ug

5 ____eep

6 ____ite

7 ____en

8 ____eans

9 ____acks

10 ____oat

11 ____ed

12 ____am

Qu qu

Queen starts with the sound of **qu**. Circle and color the pictures in each row whose names begin with the sound of **qu**.

1

2

3

4

Vv

Circle the pictures whose beginning sound is the same as the sound of the letter in the box.

I			
j			

2			
qu			

3			
v			

Say the name of each picture.

Use ▭▭▭ to color the pictures whose names start with **j**.

Use ▭▭▭ to color the pictures whose names start with **qu**.

Use ▭▭▭ to color the pictures whose names start with **v**.

Print the letter that stands for the missing sound on the line under each picture.

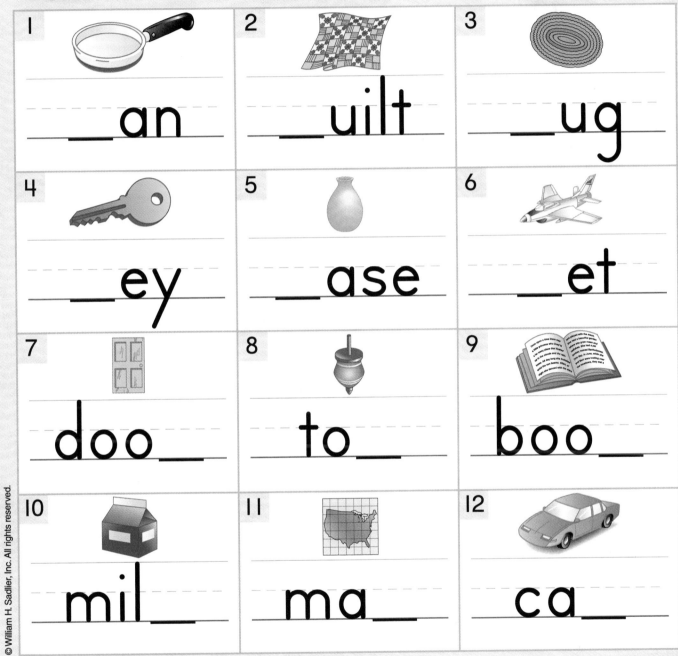

1. __an

2. __uilt

3. __ug

4. __ey

5. __ase

6. __et

7. doo__

8. to__

9. boo__

10. mil__

11. ma__

12. ca__

Cut out the letters in the boxes at the bottom of the page. Glue each letter beside a picture whose name begins with the sound of the letter.

1	2	3
4	5	6
7	8	9
10	11	12

p	p	r	r	k	k
j	j	qu	qu	v	v

The letters **Xx**, **Yy**, and **Zz** are partner letters. Find partner letters on animals in the parade. Color the animals with partner letters.

1

Xx

Xavier

f o x	m i x
w a x	X a v i e r
e x i t	b o x

2

Yasmin

Yy

y o l k	y o - y o
m a y b e	Y a s m i n
j a y	y e l l o w

3

Zz

Zach

Z a c h	Z e l d a
z e b r a	z i p p e r
z o o	f u z z y

Mix ends with the sound of **x**. Circle and color the pictures whose names end with the sound of **x**.

Xx

1	2	3	4
5	6	7	8

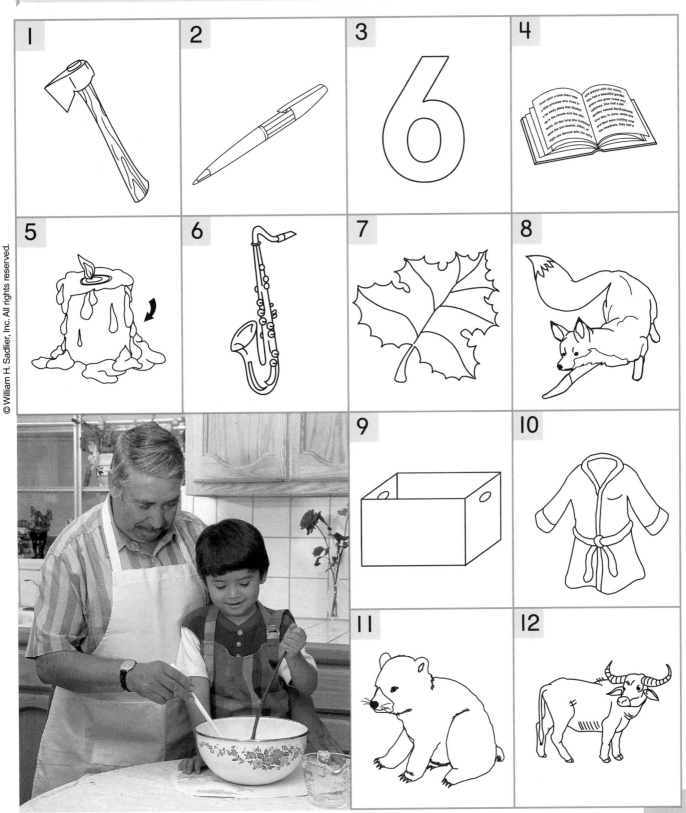

	9	10
	11	12

LESSON 36: Recognizing the Sound of Final Consonant **x**

75

The word **Yard** starts with the sound of **y**.
The word **Zebra** starts with the sound of **z**.

First circle the pictures whose names begin with the sound of **y**. Color them ⬅️.

Then circle the pictures whose names begin with the sound of **z**. Color them ⬅️.

Yy Zz

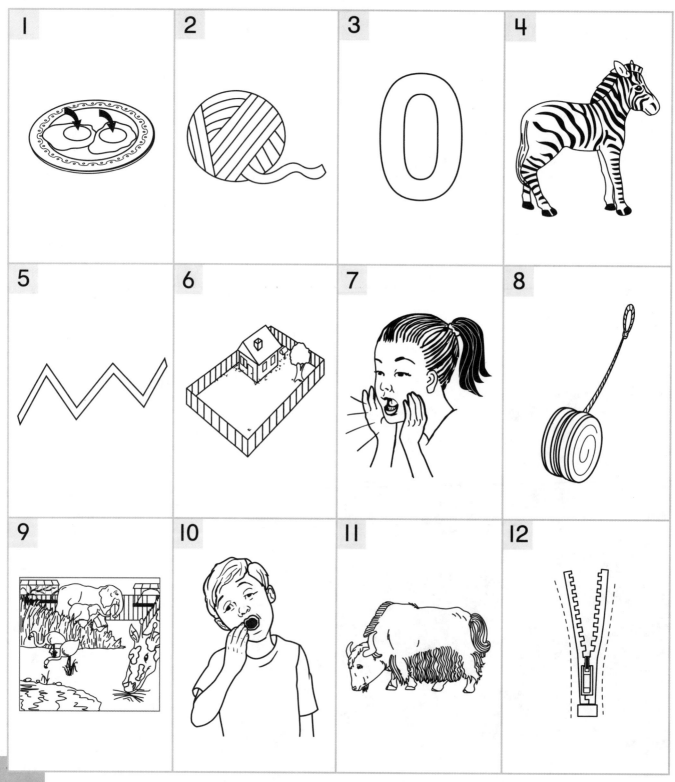

LESSON 36: Recognizing the Sounds of Initial Consonants **y** and **z**

In each game, score a tic-tac-toe by drawing a line through the three pictures whose names begin with the same sound. Print the letter that stands for the beginning sound on the winner's award.

1

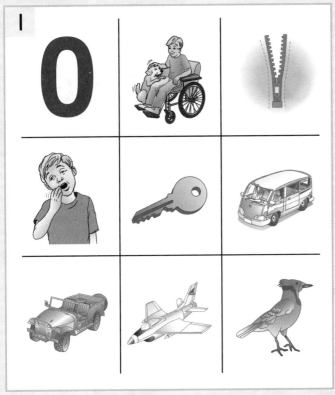

2

3

Winners

1 _ _ _ _ _ _ _ _

_ _ _ _ _ _ _ _

2 _ _ _ _ _ _ _ _

_ _ _ _ _ _ _ _

3 _ _ _ _ _ _ _ _

_ _ _ _ _ _ _ _

Check-Up Say the name of each picture. Fill in the circle before the letter that stands for the missing sound. Write the letter on the line.

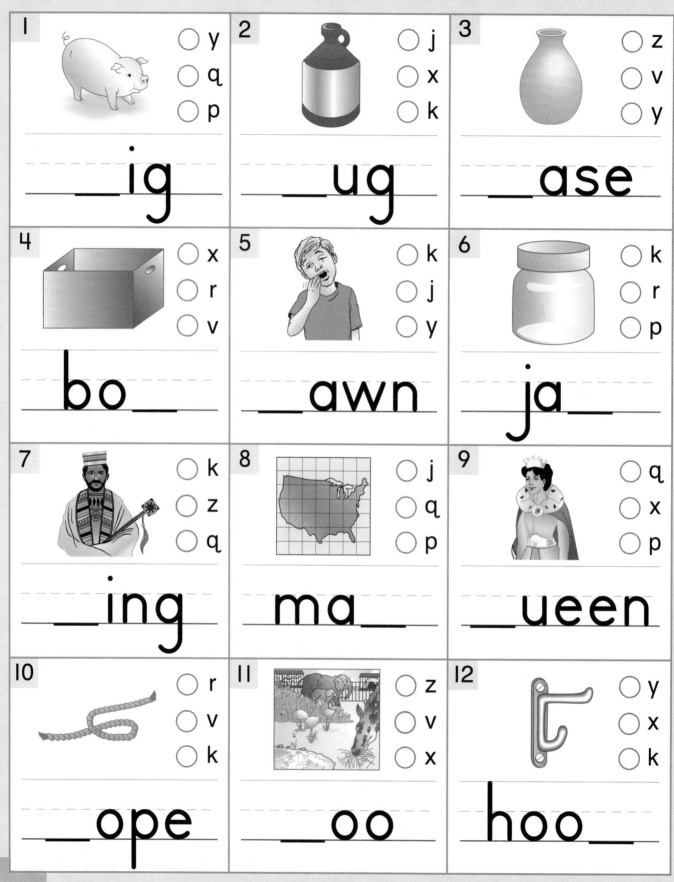

1. ○ y ○ q ○ p

__ig

2. ○ j ○ x ○ k

__ug

3. ○ z ○ v ○ y

__ase

4. ○ x ○ r ○ v

bo__

5. ○ k ○ j ○ y

__awn

6. ○ k ○ r ○ p

ja__

7. ○ k ○ z ○ q

__ing

8. ○ j ○ q ○ p

ma__

9. ○ q ○ x ○ p

__ueen

10. ○ r ○ v ○ k

__ope

11. ○ z ○ v ○ x

__oo

12. ○ y ○ x ○ k

hoo__

The middle consonant sound in **wagon** is **g**. Say the name of each picture. Circle the letter that stands for the middle consonant sound.

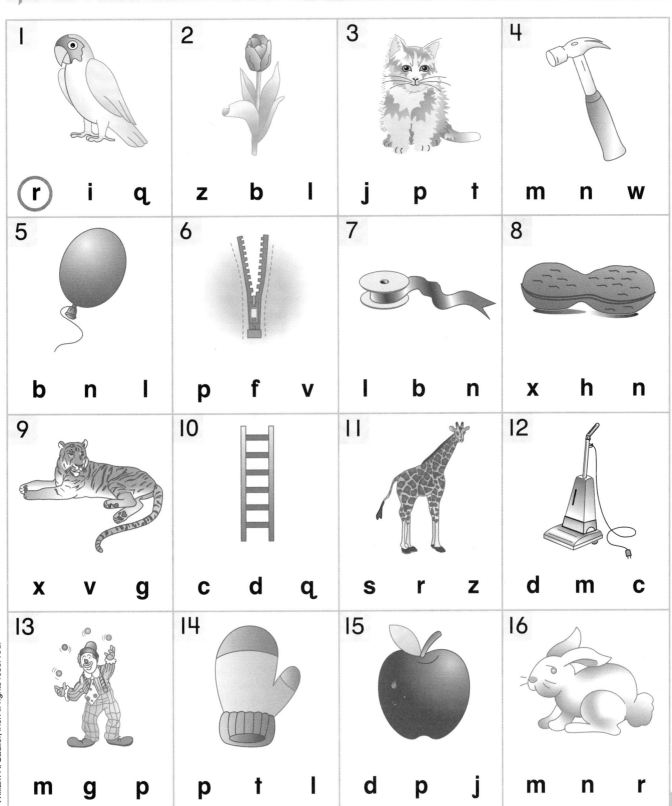

1	2	3	4
(r) i q	z b l	j p t	m n w

5	6	7	8
b n l	p f v	l b n	x h n

9	10	11	12
x v g	c d q	s r z	d m c

13	14	15	16
m g p	p t l	d p j	m n r

ay the name of each picture. Print the letter that stands for the middle consonant sound on the line.

1	2	3
wagon	spi__er	tu__ip
4	5	6
ca__el	ca__in	wa__er
7	8	9
se__en	ru__er	le__on
10	11	12
sa__ad	ro__ot	po__y

LESSON 38: Recognizing and Writing Medial Consonants

Look and Learn

Look at the pictures.
Then read and talk about them.

We can celebrate a
special time with a parade.
We can make special
food, sing special songs,
or wear special clothes.
The people in the pictures
are celebrating the new
year. Celebrations are fun!

How do you celebrate
your favorite special time?

Say the name of each picture. Print the letter that stands for the missing sound on the line.

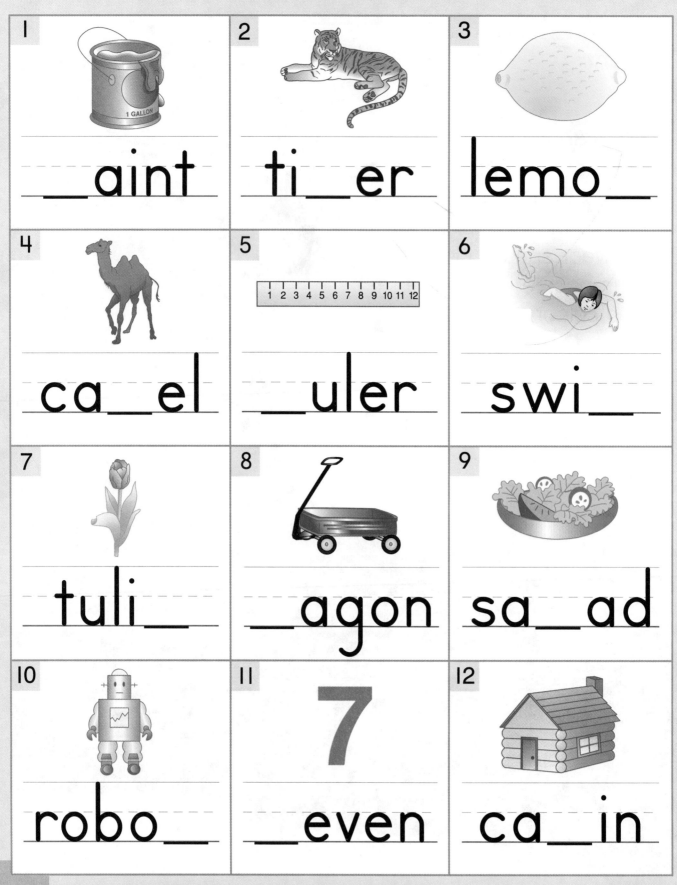

1 __aint

2 ti__er

3 lemo__

4 ca__el

5 __uler

6 swi__

7 tuli__

8 __agon

9 sa__ad

10 robo__

11 __even

12 ca__in

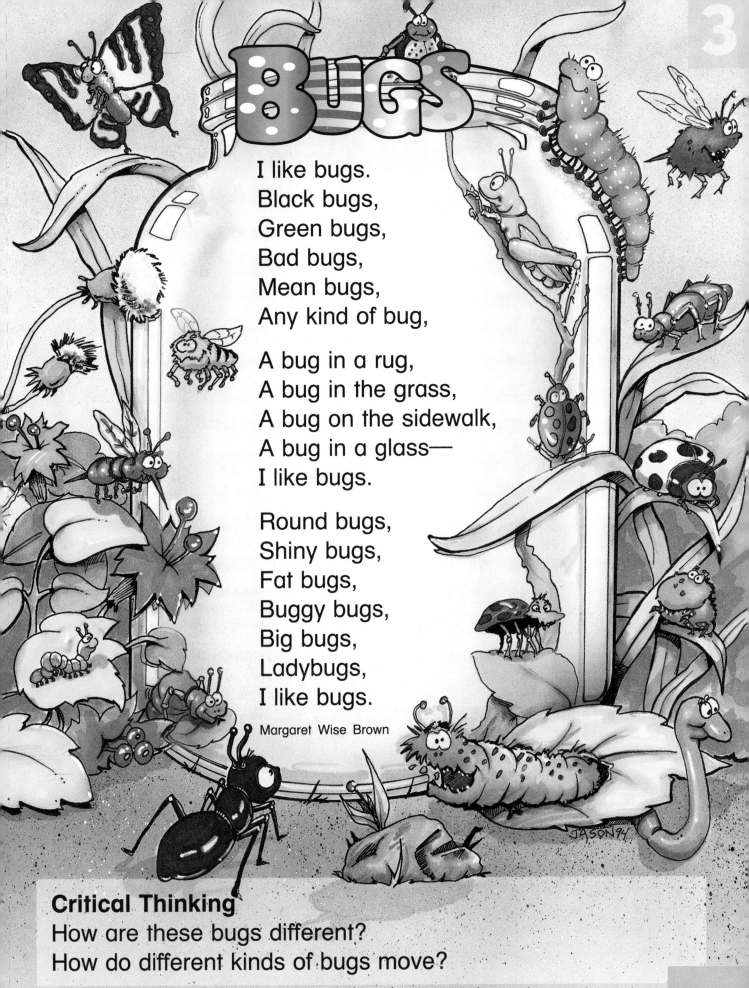

BUGS

I like bugs.
Black bugs,
Green bugs,
Bad bugs,
Mean bugs,
Any kind of bug,

A bug in a rug,
A bug in the grass,
A bug on the sidewalk,
A bug in a glass—
I like bugs.

Round bugs,
Shiny bugs,
Fat bugs,
Buggy bugs,
Big bugs,
Ladybugs,
I like bugs.

Margaret Wise Brown

Critical Thinking
How are these bugs different?
How do different kinds of bugs move?

Dear Family,

In this unit, your child will learn the sounds of the short vowels. She or he will also be thinking and reading about bugs. As your child progresses through this unit, you can make phonics come alive at home with these activities.

● Look at the pictures below. Say each letter and picture name with your child. Listen to the sound of the vowel in each word.

Apreciada Familia:

En esta unidad los niños aprenderán los sonidos cortos de las vocales. También pensarán y leerán sobre insectos. A medida que se avanza ustedes pueden revivir los fonemas en la casa con estas actividades.

● Miren los gravados. Pronuncien juntos cada letra y el nombre del objeto. Escuchen el sonido de cada vocal en la palabra.

a	i	o	u	e
	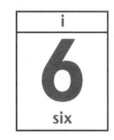	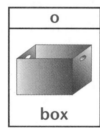	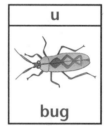	
ant	six	box	bug	ten

● Read the poem "Bugs" on the reverse side of this page as your child follows along.

● Talk about bugs. Have you ever seen a black or green bug? What could a "buggy bug" be?

● Read the poem again. Help your child find some of the short vowel words in the poem, such as **bugs, black, bad, rug, on, glass, fat**, and **big**.

● Lea el poema "Bugs" en la página 83 mientras su hijo lo repite.

● Hablen de los insectos. ¿Has visto un insecto verde o negro, alguna vez? ¿Qué puede ser un "buggy bug"?

● Lean el poema nuevamente. Ayude al niño a encontrar algunas vocales de sonido corto en las palabras del poema, tales como: **bugs, black, bad, rug, on, glass, fat** y **big**.

PROJECT

Use your imagination to draw a "never seen before" bug. Will it have spots? What kind of wings will it have? Give your new bug a name. Next to your picture, print five or six words that describe it.

PROYECTO

Dibujen un "insecto nunca visto". ¿Tendrá motitas? ¿Qué tipo de alas tendrá? Pónganle un nombre al nuevo insecto. Escriban cinco o seis palabras para describirlo.

I Can

I **can pack** a **bag.**
An ant can't.

I **can tag** a **pal.**
An ant can't.

I **can clap** my **hands.**
An ant can't.

I **can** hide in the **grass.**
And an ant can, too!

Ant has the short **a** sound. Circle and color each picture whose name has the short **a** sound.

a

1	2	3	4
5	6	7	8
9	10	11	12
13	14	15	16

LESSON 41: Recognizing the Sound of Short Vowel **a**

Say the name of each picture. Circle the pictures whose names rhyme. Then make a new rhyming word.

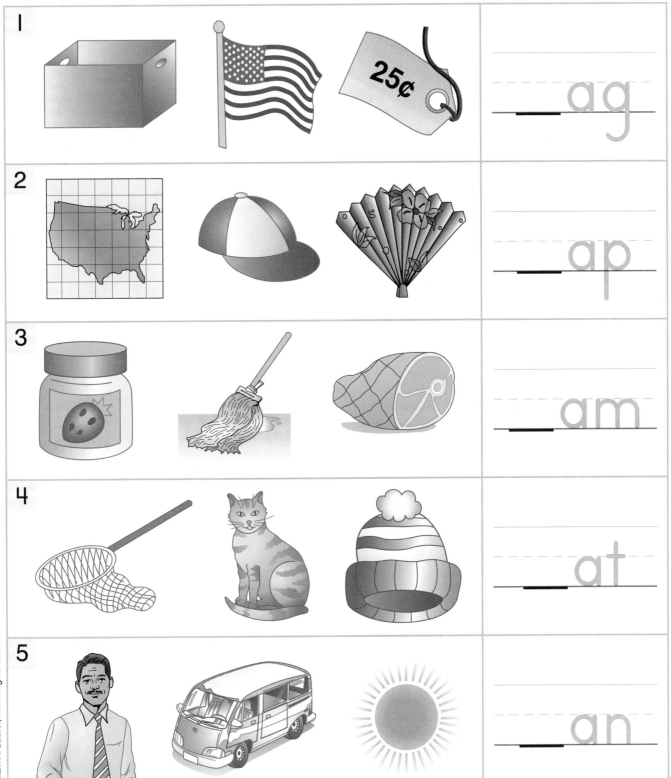

1. _____ ag

2. _____ ap

3. _____ am

4. _____ at

5. _____ an

LESSON 42: Short Vowel **a** Phonograms

87

Trace the line as you sound and say each word. Print the word on the line. Then circle the picture it names.

1

b ag bag

2

c ap

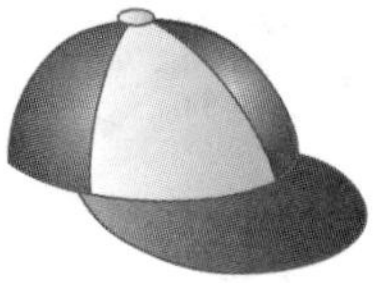

3

c an

4

h am

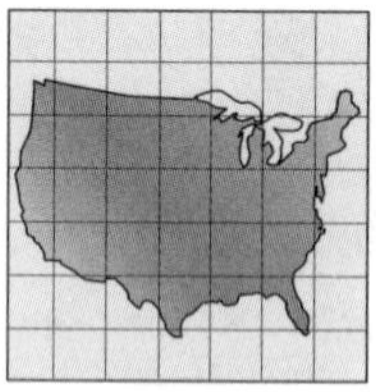

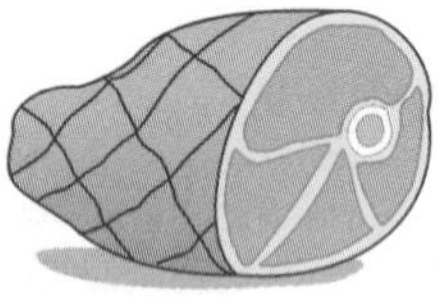

5

b at

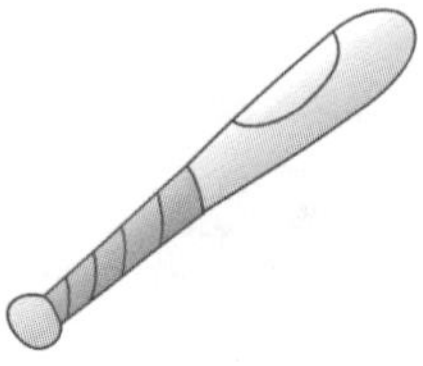

6

v an

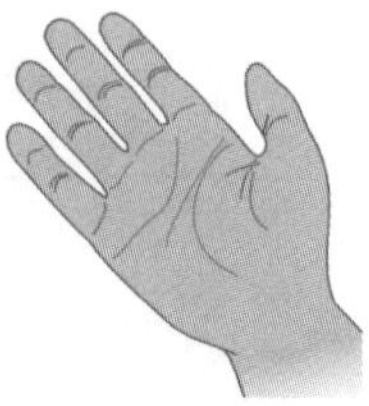

LESSON 42: Blending with Phonograms

Trace the line as you sound and say each word. Then print the word under the picture it names.

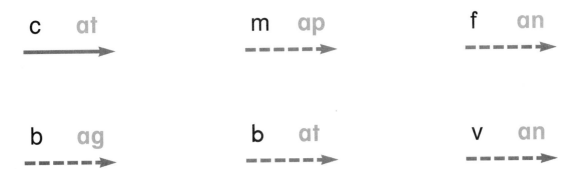

c   at   m   ap   f   an

b   ag   b   at   v   an

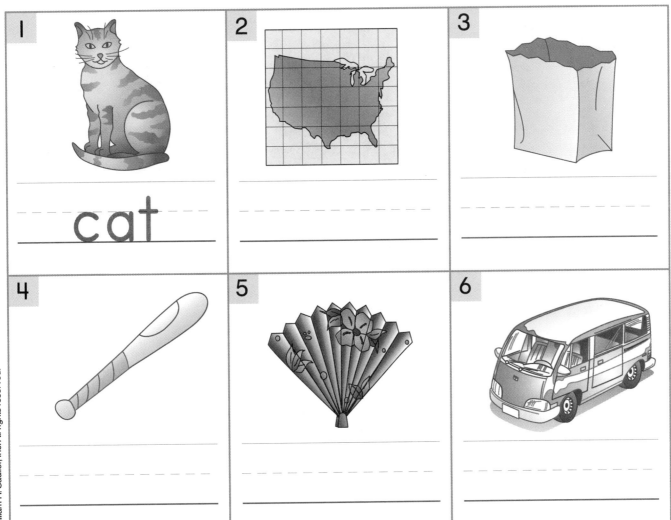

1. cat

2.

3.

4.

5.

6.

Say each word part. Say the name of each picture. Print the word on the line. Then add your own rhyming word and picture.

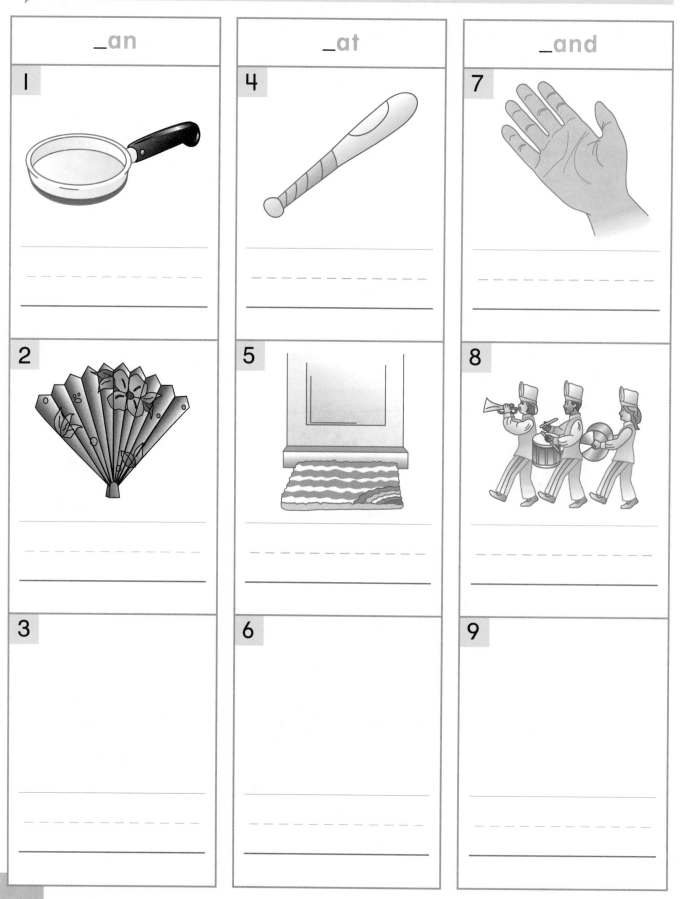

_an	_at	_and
1	4	7
2	5	8
3	6	9

Say the name of each picture. Circle the word and print it on the line.

1	fat tan **(fan)**	2	ham hat jam	3	and ant ax
	fan				

4	can cat ran	5	band pat bat	6	pal pan plan

7	rap map pad	8	camp cat sat	9	land damp hand

10	bag bad grab	11	tap cab cap	12	tag rag tab

1

Dan got his __bat__.

fat
(bat)
bad

2

He _____ up the hill.

rap
pan
ran

3

His _____ fell off.

cap
cat
can

4

Dan _____ on the log.

sat
rat
mat

5

He felt a bug on his _____.

ham
sand
hand

6

It was just a little _____.

ax
ant
tan

Read the poem. Then use short **a** words to complete the sentences.

My Ant Farm

My pet ants
Snack on jam.
Their names are
Ann, Nat, and Sam.

I hand them
Scraps and grass.
Then I watch them
In the glass.

1. Jam is a _____ for the ants.

2. The ants are Ann, Nat, and _____.

3. You can watch them in the _____.

Use the pictures to complete the puzzle. Start in the box with the same number as the clue. Print one letter in each box.

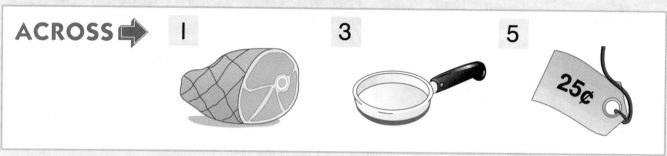

ACROSS ➡   1 [ham]   3 [pan]   5 [tag]

DOWN ⬇

2 [map]

4 [ant]

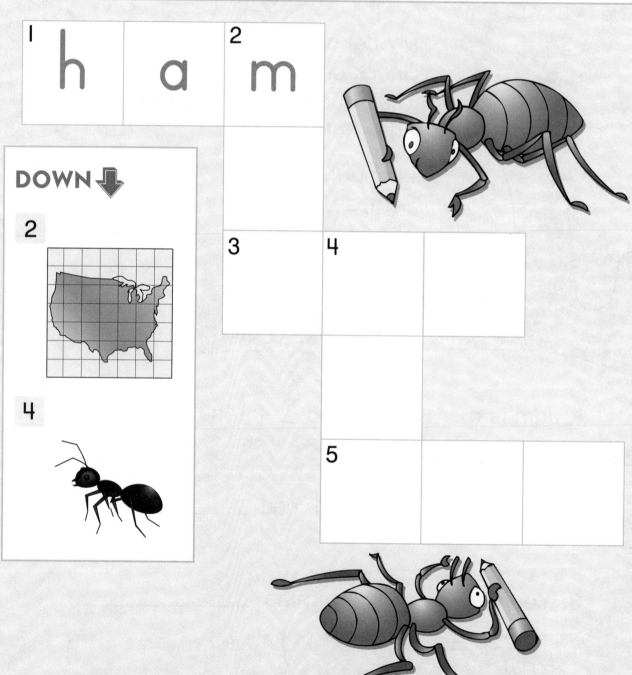

1 h	a	2 m

94   LESSON 45: Reviewing Short Vowel a

Read the poem together. Underline the short **i** words. Draw the answer to the riddle at the bottom of the page.

What Is It?

It has **six** legs,
And **it** has **wings**.
Sometimes **it sits**.
Sometimes **it stings**.

What **is it**?

It is a **big**

Six has the short **i** sound. Circle and color each picture whose name has the short **i** sound.

6

i

LESSON 46: Recognizing the Sound of Short Vowel **i**

Say the name of each picture. Circle the pictures whose names rhyme. Then make a new rhyming word.

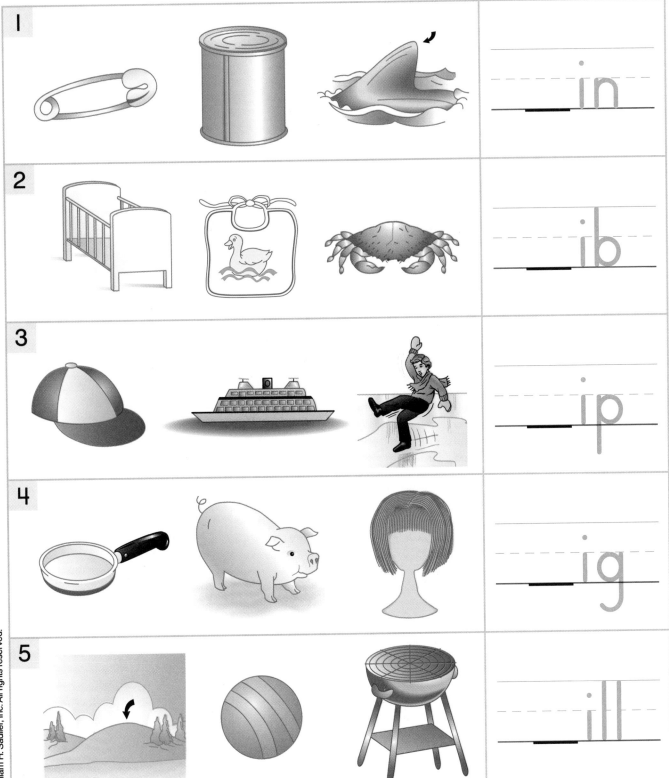

1   ___ in

2   ___ ib

3   ___ ip

4   ___ ig

5   ___ ill

LESSON 47: Short Vowel **i** Phonograms

97

1	2	3
f in - - - →	b ib - - - →	p in - - - →

4	5	6
l id - - - →	s ix - - - → **6**	w ig - - - →

7	8	9
m ix - - - →	d ig - - - →	r ip - - - →

Trace the line as you sound and say each word. Print the word on the line. Then circle the picture it names.

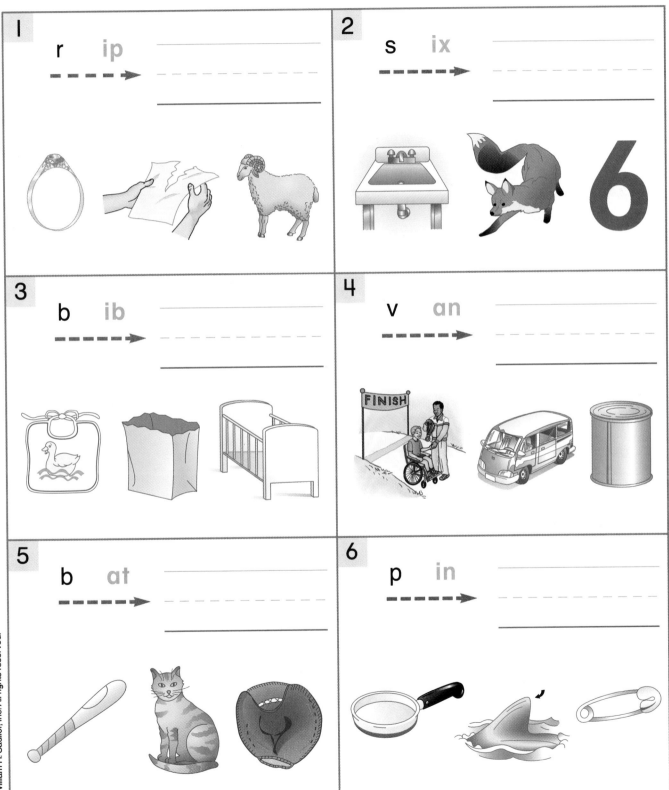

1. r ip

2. s ix

3. b ib

4. v an

5. b at

6. p in

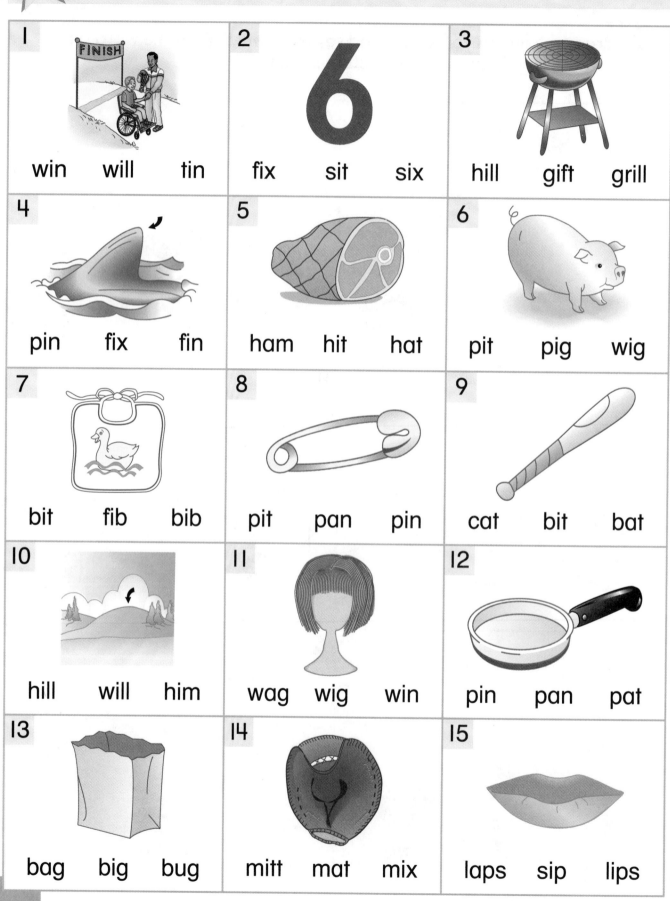

C ircle the word that names each picture.

1 win will tin	**2** fix sit six	**3** hill gift grill
4 pin fix fin	**5** ham hit hat	**6** pit pig wig
7 bit fib bib	**8** pit pan pin	**9** cat bit bat
10 hill will him	**11** wag wig win	**12** pin pan pat
13 bag big bug	**14** mitt mat mix	**15** laps sip lips

1	cab crab (crib)	2	lid hid lad	3	sat six sit
	crib				

4	can call sand	5	mitt mill mat	6	big will wig

7	mix map mitt	8	pig pat pin	9	dad dig did

10	lips laps sips	11	tag pill pig	12	ham hit hill

ay the name of each picture. Print it on the line.

1

bib

2

3

4

5

6

7

8

9

10

11

12

13

14

15

16

Look at the picture. Circle the word that completes the sentence. Print it on the line.

1		Lin __sits__ still.	hits six (sits)
2		A bug _____ in the grass.	is kiss as
3		Lin is _____ to grab it.	bib sink quick
4		Lin has the bug _____ the jar.	is in it
5		Lin looks at _____ .	it in an
6		She lifts the _____ .	lad lid Lin

LESSON 50: Short Vowel **i** in Sentences

103

What Is a Bug?

Some bugs have six legs,
Not more than six!
Some bugs have odd names,
Like walking sticks.

Insects can have wings,
And some can sting!
It seems bugs can do
All kinds of things.

1. Some bugs have _____ legs.

2. Bugs with _____ can fly.

3. Look out for bugs that can _____.

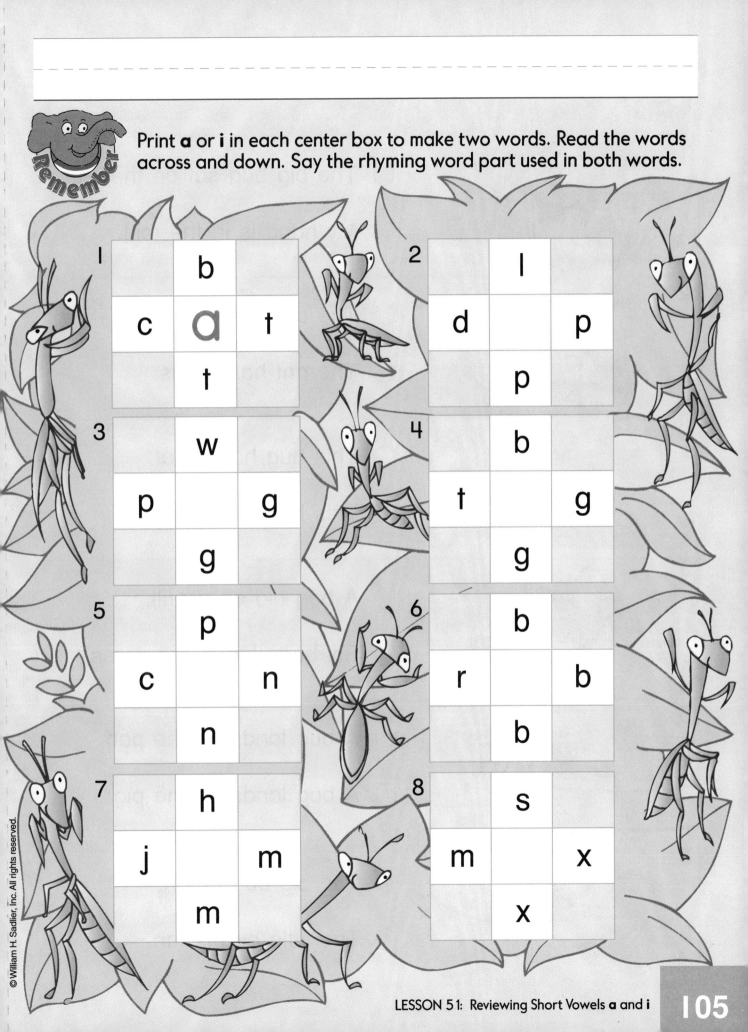

Print **a** or **i** in each center box to make two words. Read the words across and down. Say the rhyming word part used in both words.

1 | b | | |
c | a | t
| t |

2 | | l | |
d | | p
| p |

3 | w | |
p | | g
| g |

4 | b | |
t | | g
| g |

5 | p | |
c | | n
| n |

6 | b | |
r | | b
| b |

7 | h | |
j | | m
| m |

8 | s | |
m | | x
| x |

LESSON 51: Reviewing Short Vowels **a** and **i**   105

Read the sentences. Fill in the circle before the one that tells about the picture.

1	○ The big bug sat on the mitt.
	○ My hand is in the mitt.
2	○ The ant can dig.
	○ The ant has wings.
3	○ This bug has a hat.
	○ This bug will sting.
4	○ A bug hid on a grill.
	○ Six bugs hid in the grass.
5	○ A bug lands on the pan.
	○ A bug lands on the pig.
6	○ The big bug is tan.
	○ The little bug is tan.

Read the story together. Draw a line under the short **o** words. Then act out the story.

Hop and Stop

Hop! Hop! Hop!
Time to **stop**.

Hop to the **box**.
Time to **stop**.

Jog in place.
Time to **stop**.

Isn't it fun
To **hop** and **stop!**

Box has the short **o** sound. Print **o** on the line under the pictures whose names have the short **o** sound.

O

1	2	3	4
5	6	7	8
9	10	11	12
13	14	15	16

LESSON 52: Recognizing the Sound of Short Vowel **o**

Say the name of each picture. Circle the pictures whose names rhyme. Then make a new rhyming word.

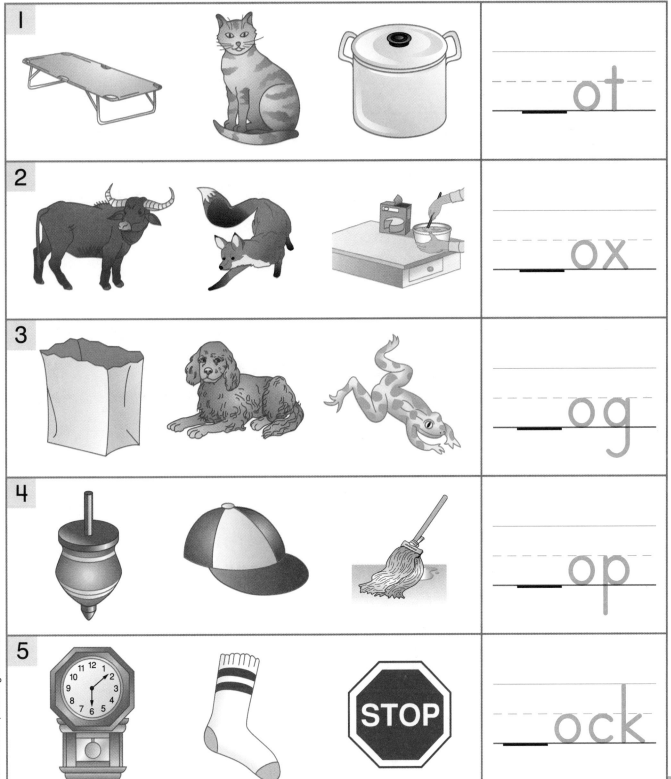

1. ___ot

2. ___ox

3. ___og

4. ___op

5. ___ock

1

m op _____

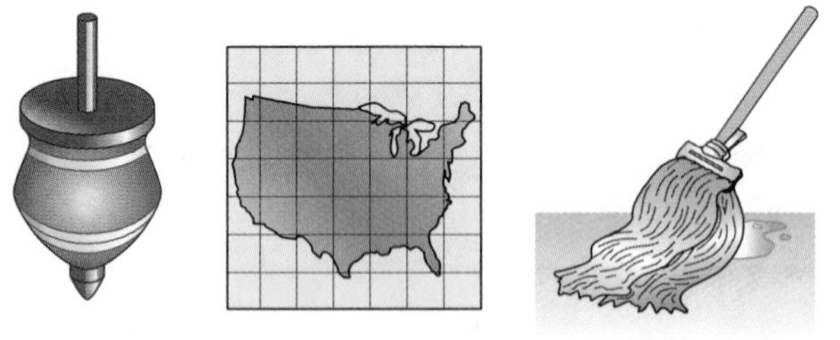

2

c ob _____

3

p op _____

4

b ox _____

5

d og _____

6

h ot _____

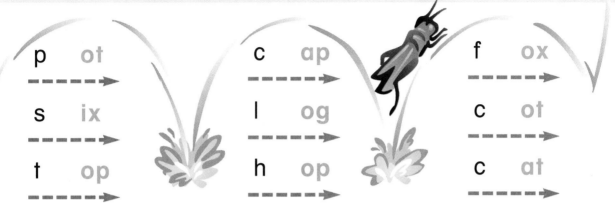

p ot - - - →

s ix - - - →

t op - - - →

c ap - - - →

l og - - - →

h op - - - →

f ox - - - →

c ot - - - →

c at - - - →

1	2	3
6		

4	5	6

7	8	9

Say each word part. Say the name of each picture. Print the word on the line. Then add your own rhyming word and picture.

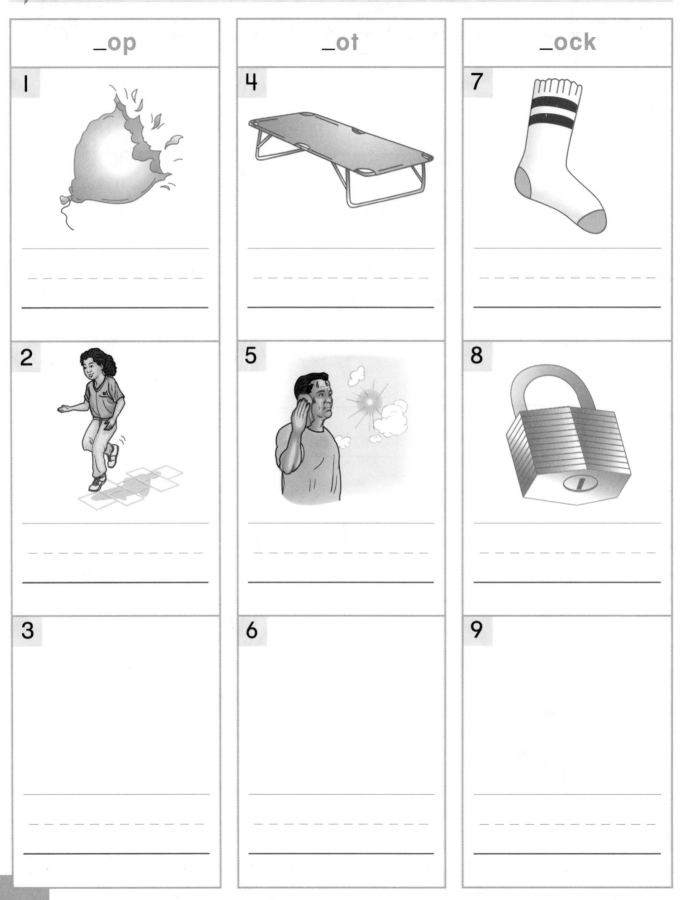

_op	_ot	_ock
1	4	7
2	5	8
3	6	9

LESSON 54: Short Vowel o Phonograms

Circle the word that names each picture.

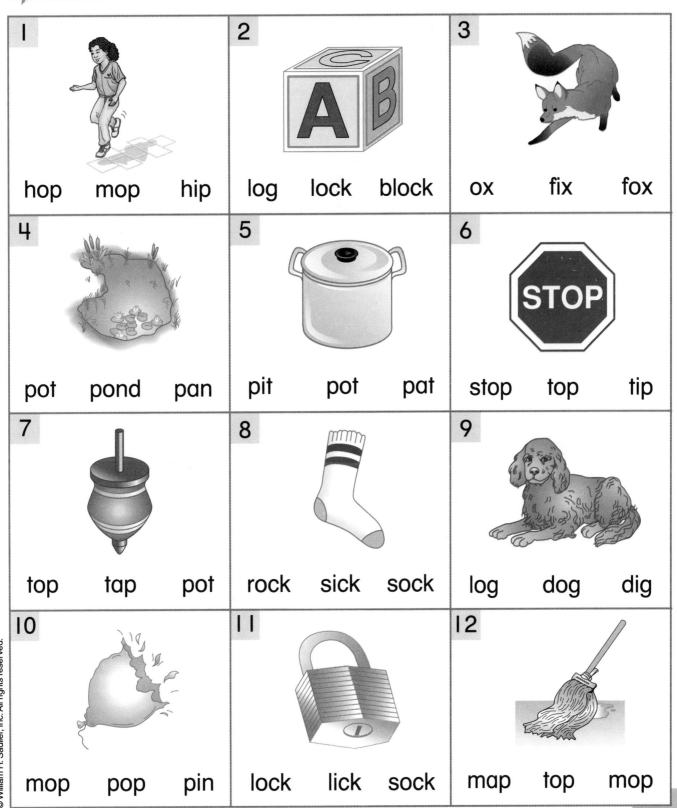

1 hop mop hip	**2** log lock block	**3** ox fix fox
4 pot pond pan	**5** pit pot pat	**6** stop top tip
7 top tap pot	**8** rock sick sock	**9** log dog dig
10 mop pop pin	**11** lock lick sock	**12** map top mop

1
fog
dig
frog

_____

2
ox
ax
box

_____

3
pit
pop
mop

_____

4
cob
cat
cot

_____

5
wig
wag
win

_____

6
rock
back
lock

_____

7
top
map
mop

_____

8
hit
hat
hot

_____

9
mop
man
mat

_____

10
tap
tip
top

_____

11
rock
sock
rack

_____

12
hit
hill
hot

_____

Look at each picture. Then print the correct sentence part on the line.

| on the log. | on the rock. | on the top. |
| in the sock. | in the box. | |

1 Where is the bug?

It is on the top.

2 Where is the bug?

It is _____

3 Where is the bug?

It is _____

4 Where is the bug?

It is _____

5 Where is the bug?

It is _____

Read the story. Look at the picture. Number the sentences to show the correct order.

Hop, Bug, Hop!

Hop, Bug, hop!
Hop past Pop.
Hop to the blocks.
Hop in the box.
Hop over the dog.
Hop up on the log.

Stop, Bug, stop!
Don't hop in the pond.

_____ The bug hops over the dog.

_____ The bug hops to the blocks.

_____ The bug hops past Pop.

_____ The bug hops up on the log.

_____ The bug hops in the box.

Read the words in the box. Color the picture each word names.

fox	log	rock	hat
pond	man	fin	frog

Check-Up Read the sentences. Fill in the circle before the one that tells about the picture.

1

○ The bug is on the log.

○ The bug is on my hat.

2

○ This bug can not hop.

○ This bug can hop.

3

○ The dog nips at the bug.

○ The bug is on the ox.

4

○ The ant sits on the hill.

○ Six ants sit on the hill.

5

○ The bug hid from the frog.

○ The frog hops to the pond.

6

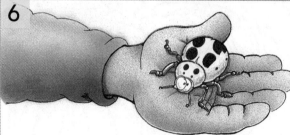

○ The bug is in a bag.

○ The bug is in his hand.

LESSON 57: Assessing Short Vowels **a, i, o**

Read the poem together. Draw a line under the short **u** words. Then color the bugs.

A Snug Bug

One little **bug**
In the middle of a **rug**.
Poor little **bug**
Isn't very **snug**.

Tug, **bug**, **tug**!
Roll up the **rug**.
Soon you'll be
Cozy and **snug**.

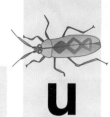

Bug has the short **u** sound. Circle and color each picture whose name has the short **u** sound.

u

1 	2	3	4
5	6	7	8
9	10	11	12
13	14	15	16

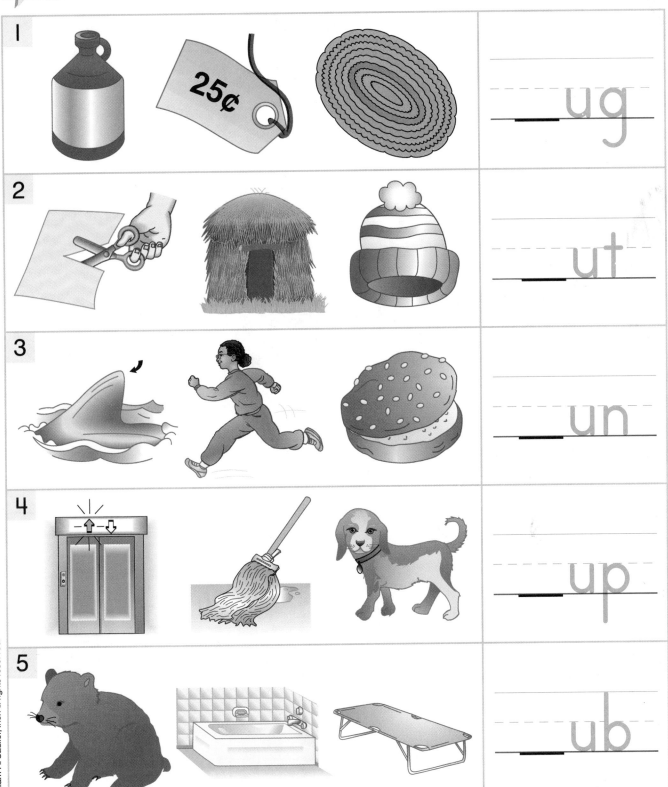

Say the name of each picture. In each row, circle the pictures whose names rhyme. Then make a new rhyming word.

1				___ug
2				___ut
3				___un
4				___up
5				___ub

1

c ub

- - - →

2

h ut

- - - →

3

t ub

- - - →

4

b us

- - - →

5

b un

- - - →

6

n ut

- - - →

7

r ug

- - - →

8

c up

- - - →

9

h ug

- - - →

Trace the line as you sound and say each word. Then print the word on the line in the correct sentence.

b ug

s un

c ub

p up

b ud

1. The bug sits in the hot _____.

2. It sees a _____ in the grass.

3. It sees a _____, too.

4. The __bug__ must run fast.

5. The bug is snug in the _____.

LESSON 60: Blending and Using Phonograms in Sentences

123

Circle the word that names each picture.

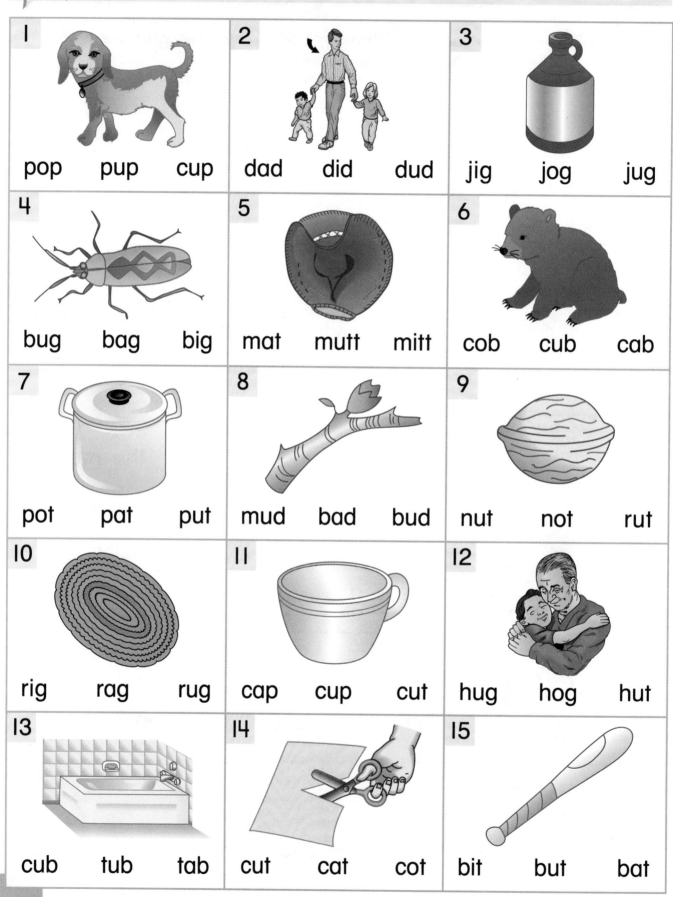

1	2	3
pop pup cup	dad did dud	jig jog jug
4	5	6
bug bag big	mat mutt mitt	cob cub cab
7	8	9
pot pat put	mud bad bud	nut not rut
10	11	12
rig rag rug	cap cup cut	hug hog hut
13	14	15
cub tub tab	cut cat cot	bit but bat

Say the name of each picture. Circle the word and print it on the line.

1 tub cub cob	**2** bit band bun	**3** hut hat hot
4 dock duck rock	**5** nut cut not	**6** and fun fan
7 bus bug gas	**8** hill hot hit	**9** sun run ran
10 drop ram drum	**11** pig log pup	**12** grab bug big

LESSON 61: Practicing Short Vowel **u**

125

ay the name of each picture. Print it on the line.

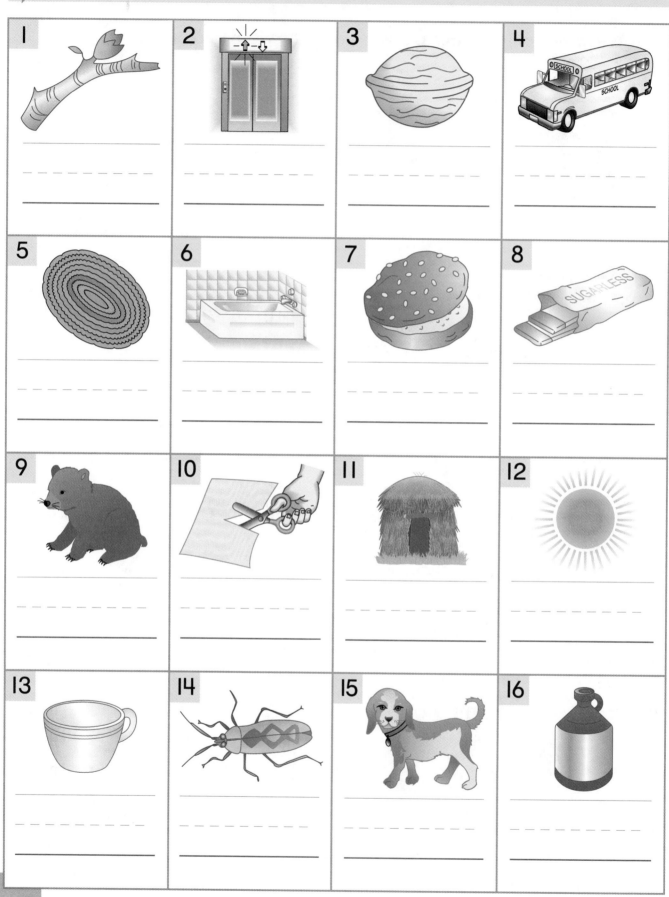

Look at the picture. Circle the word that completes the sentence. Print it on the line.

1	The _____ naps on the log.	cub cap cut
2	"Buzz," _____ the bug.	has hams hums
3	The cub looks _____ at it.	us up as
4	It bats at the _____.	bag beg bug
5	This is not _____.	fit fun fat
6	The cub _____ off.	runs suns funs

A Buggy Lunch

Lunch with bugs
Is not fun!
A bug is in the cup.
A bug is on the bun.
Bugs bug us!
Run, bugs, run.

Yuck!

1. Bugs are not _____ at lunch.

2. A bug is in the _____.

3. A bug is on the _____.

4. Bugs _____ us. Yuck!

Find the hidden three-letter words. Circle them. Then print the vowels that will complete the words on the lines.

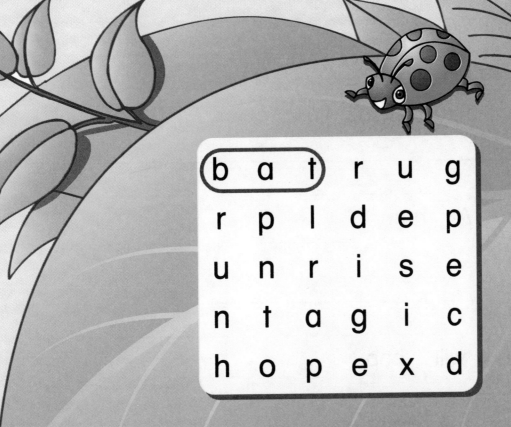

b	a	t	r	u	g
r	p	l	d	e	p
u	n	r	i	s	e
n	t	a	g	i	c
h	o	p	e	x	d

1. b a t

2. r _ g

3. h _ p

4. r _ n

5. s _ x

6. t _ g

Unscramble the words to make a sentence.
Write the sentence on the line.

1   buzz? a Can bug

_____

2   a run? Can bug

_____

3   pup can A run.

_____

4   bug This will hop.

_____

5   pig a Will hop?

_____

6   nap. dog a had The

_____

LESSON 63: Reviewing Short Vowels **a, i, o, u**

Read the poem together. Say the names of the things under the bed. Color them Ted's favorite color, red.

It's **Ted** the bug.
His room's a **mess**.
He has **ten** things
Not more, not **less**.

He hid his things
Under his **bed**.
And all the things
Ted hid are **red**.

Ten has the short **e** sound. Circle and color each picture whose name has the short **e** sound.

LESSON 64: Recognizing the Sound of Short Vowel **e**

1 ___en

2 ___ell

3 ___et

4 ___ed

5 ___est

Trace the line as you sound and say each word. Print the word on the line. Then circle the picture it names.

1

h **en** _____

- - - - - ▸ _ _ _ _ _ _ _ _ _

_____

2

p **et** _____

- - - - - ▸ _ _ _ _ _ _ _ _ _

_____

3

b **ed** _____

- - - - - ▸ _ _ _ _ _ _ _ _ _

_____

4

n **et** _____

- - - - - ▸ _ _ _ _ _ _ _ _ _

_____

5

m **en** _____

- - - - - ▸ _ _ _ _ _ _ _ _ _

_____

6

l **eg** _____

- - - - - ▸ _ _ _ _ _ _ _ _ _

_____

LESSON 65: Blending with Phonograms

Trace the line as you sound and say each word. Then print the word on the correct line.

t en ---->

b et ---->

h en ---->

g et ---->

v et ---->

1. Red is a big _____.

2. The _____ sees Red in her nest.

3. The nest has _____ eggs in it.

4. Peck, peck. Can Red _____ a bug?

5. I'll _____ she can!

Say each word part. Say the name of each picture. Print the word on the line. Then add your own rhyming word and picture.

_en	_et	_ell
1	**4**	**7**
2	**5**	**8**
3	**6**	**9**

Circle the word that names each picture.

1 net · not · nut	**2** 10 ten · tin · tan	**3** wig · wet · wax
4 belt · bat · bell	**5** nuts · rest · nest	**6** pen · pin · pan
7 rid · rod · red	**8** ten · tent · tint	**9** beg · big · bag
10 will · well · went	**11** hem · ham · hum	**12** jam · jot · jet
13 pup · pep · pop	**14** vest · van · vet	**15** bad · bid · bed

Say the name of each picture. Circle the word and print it on the line.

1
hen
den
dim

2
net
rut
nut

3
bill
bull
bell

4
ten
tent
tin

5
disk
desk
dent

6
pet
pit
pot

7
bag
leg
let

8
man
met
men

9
bit
bat
bet

10
pen
pin
pan

11
dig
dog
den

12
lap
let
log

LESSON 67: Practicing Short Vowel **e**

Look at the picture. Circle the word that completes the sentence. Print it on the line.

1

Can a bug be a _____ ?

pat
pet
pot

2

_____ , it can.

Yes
Yet
Jet

3

It can be the _____ pet.

list
best
rest

4

It will not be a _____ .

last
past
pest

5

It will not make a _____ .

mess
miss
moss

6

But it must be _____ .

fan
fin
fed

The Big Bug Race

Get set, bugs.
Bend six legs.
Run past the hen.
Run past the pen.
Run past the men.
Run, bugs, run.
Run to the end.

_____

1. The bugs run past the _____.

_____

2. They run past the _____.

_____

3. They run past the _____.

_____

4. They will run to the _____.

Spell and Write

Say and spell each word in the box. Then print each word under the vowel sound in its name.

bug	
six	
bed	
hat	
log	
fun	
sit	
get	
had	
not	

Short a

1 hat

2 _____

Short u

7 _____

8 _____

Short i

3 _____

4 _____

Short e

9 _____

10 _____

Short o

5 _____

6 _____

 **Spell and Write** Write a sentence about each picture. Use one or more of your new spelling words in each sentence.

bug	bed	log	sit	had
six	hat	fun	get	not

1

_____

_____

_____

_____

_____

_____

2

_____

_____

_____

_____

_____

_____

Use the picture clues to complete the puzzles.
Print one letter in each box.

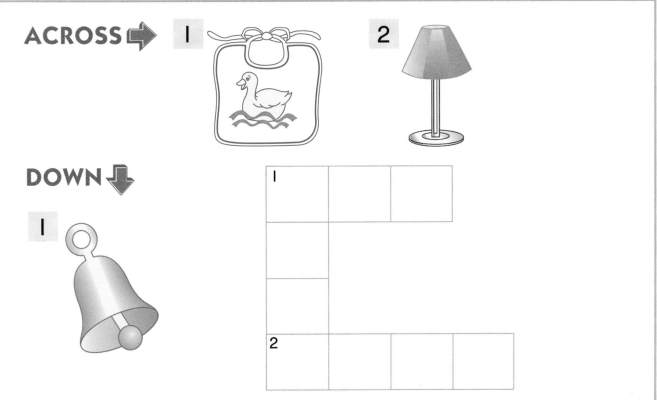

ACROSS ➡ 1 [bib] 2 [lamp]

DOWN ⬇ 1 [bell]

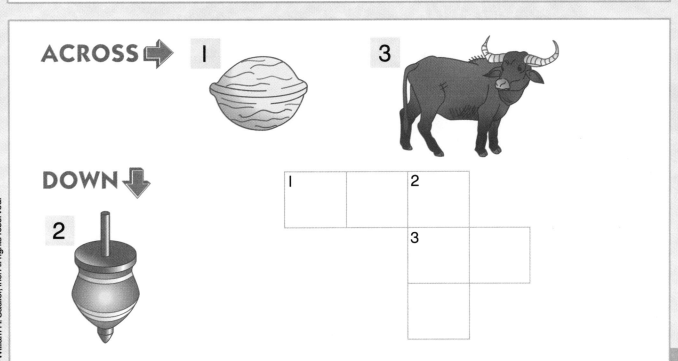

ACROSS ➡ 1 [nut] 3 [ox]

DOWN ⬇ 2 [top]

LESSON 70: Reviewing Short Vowels **a, i, o, u, e**   143

Read the words in the boxes. Combine words from boxes 1, 2, and 3 to make sentences. Print them on the lines. How many sentences can you make?

1	2	3
Six bugs	had fun	at the pond.
A frog	will jump	in the sun.
The bug	can hop	on the bud.

Look at the pictures. Then read and talk about them.

Can you spot the bugs?
Don't let them trick you.
They can see you just fine.
Lots of bugs blend in well with
rocks, plants, and sticks.
The bugs can sit still for a very
long time. This helps them hide
and stay safe.

What else can bugs do?

Treehopper

Walkingstick

Katydid

LESSON 7 1: Short Vowels in Context **145**

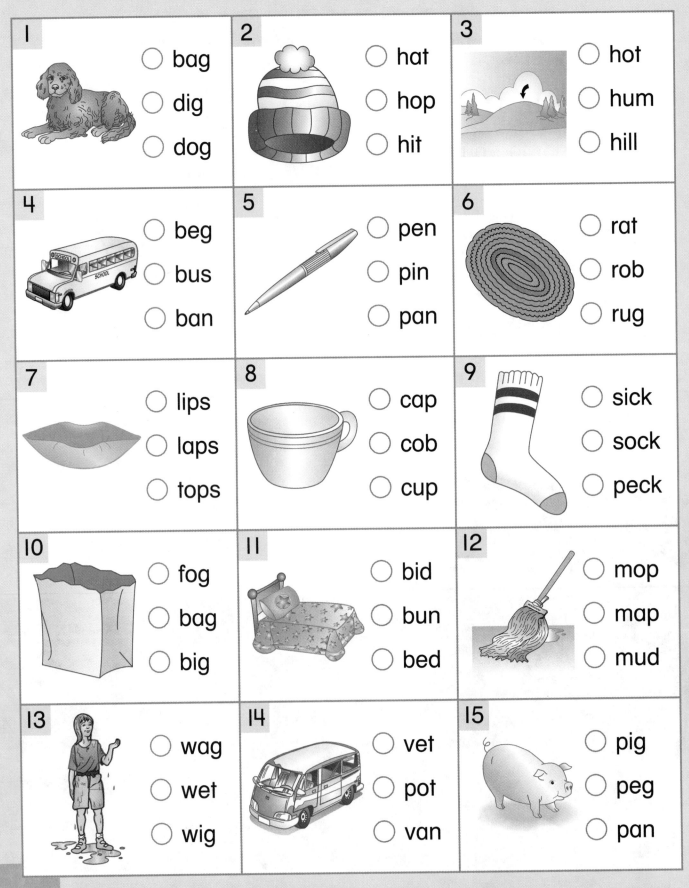

1
○ bag
○ dig
○ dog

2
○ hat
○ hop
○ hit

3
○ hot
○ hum
○ hill

4
○ beg
○ bus
○ ban

5
○ pen
○ pin
○ pan

6
○ rat
○ rob
○ rug

7
○ lips
○ laps
○ tops

8
○ cap
○ cob
○ cup

9
○ sick
○ sock
○ peck

10
○ fog
○ bag
○ big

11
○ bid
○ bun
○ bed

12
○ mop
○ map
○ mud

13
○ wag
○ wet
○ wig

14
○ vet
○ pot
○ van

15
○ pig
○ peg
○ pan

YESTERDAY'S PAPER

Yesterday's paper makes a hat,
　Or a boat,
　Or a plane,
　Or a playhouse mat.

Yesterday's paper makes things
Like that—
And a very fine tent
For a sleeping cat.

Mabel Watts

Critical Thinking

What else could you make out of old newspapers?
How might you recycle other things?

Dear Family,

As your child learns about our environment in this unit, he or she will also be learning the sounds of the long vowels. As your child progresses through the unit, you can participate by trying these activities together at home.

● Look at the pictures below. Say each letter and picture name with your child. Listen for the long vowel sounds. (Long vowels say their own name.)

a	i	o	u	e
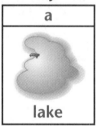				
lake	bike	toad	mule	tree

● Read the poem "Yesterday's Paper" on the reverse side of this page.

● Talk about ways to recycle, or to use again, such things as paper, cans, toys, and even clothes that have been outgrown.

● Help your child find long vowel words in the poem, such as **paper**, **makes**, **boat**, **plane**, **playhouse**, **like**, **fine**, and **sleeping**.

Apreciada Familia:

Mientras aprenden sobre el medio ambiente los niños también aprenderán el sonido largo de las vocales. Mientras su hijo avanza pueden participar de estas actividades en el hogar.

● Miren los siguientes cuadros. Pronuncien cada letra y el nombre del objeto. Escuchen el sonido largo de las vocales. (El sonido es el de su nombre).

● Lean el poema "Yesterday's Paper" en la página 147.

● Hablen de las diferentes formas de recircular, o usar de nuevo, algunas cosas como papel, latas, juguetes, ropa que ya quedan pequeñas o pasadas de moda.

● Ayuden al niño a encontrar vocales de sonido fuerte en el poema, tales como: **paper**, **makes**, **boat**, **plane**, **playhouse**, **like**, **fine** y **sleeping**.

PROJECT

Recycle an old shoe box and some used magazines or catalogs. Help your child cut out magazine pictures of things that have long vowel sounds in their names. Put the pictures in the box. Ask your child to sort the pictures according to the different long vowel sounds.

PROYECTO

Recirculen una caja de zapatos. Pida al niño recortar de revistas fotos de cosas que tengan vocales de sonido largo en sus nombres. Pongan las fotos en la caja. El niño puede ordenarlas de acuerdo a los diferentes sonidos.

Read the poem together. Draw a line under the long **a** words. Color the pictures that show someone who is saving the earth.

Save the Earth

Save the **snakes**.
Save the **whales**.
Save the blue **jays**.
Save the **snails**.

Save the **lakes**.
Save the **bays**.
You can help
In many **ways**.

Lake has the long **a** sound. Circle and color each picture whose name has the long **a** sound.

a

1	2	3	4
5	6	7	8
9	10	11	12
13	14	15	16

LESSON 73: Recognizing the Sound of Long Vowel **a**

1   ___ ake

2   ___ ate

3   ___ ail

4   ___ age

5   ___ ay

Say the name of each picture. Color in each box which has a rhyming word.

1

jay

day	say
game	hay

2

sail

mail	vase
pail	tail

3

lake

tape	cake
bake	take

4

cave

wave	gave
Dave	nail

5

gate

snail	skate
date	late

6

rain

train	brain
safe	gain

7

stage

cage	cape
date	page

8

game

tame	same
came	vase

Say each word part. Say the name of each picture. Print the word on the line. Then add your own rhyming word and picture.

_ay	_ake	_ail
1	4	7
2	5	8
3	6	9

Circle the word that names each picture.

1	**2**	**3**
ran rain rail	frame from fall	cake can cage
4	**5**	**6**
will whale wall	hay hat hill	safe same sat
7	**8**	**9**
plate late pat	stage stain age	rock ram rake
10	**11**	**12**
tape tap tip	top train tan	jet pay jay
13	**14**	**15**
saw sell sail	tray trap trip	can cane cot

LESSON 75: Recognizing Long Vowel **a**

Say the name of each picture. Circle the word and print it on the line.

1	lamp lake late	2	gate get game	3	take tell tail
4	wait well wave	5	cape cap car	6	jay jet gas
7	game gum gaze	8	name nail net	9	vane van vase
10	man make mail	11	sell sail same	12	cat sock cake

1 cape	2 cap	3 pay	4 bat
L S	L S	L S	L S
5 sail	6 cane	7 lake	8 can
L S	L S	L S	L S
9 jay	10 pan	11 hat	12 rain
L S	L S	L S	L S
13 hay	14 bag	15 jacks	16 gate
L S	L S	L S	L S

Look at the picture. Circle the word that completes the sentence. Print it on the line.

1	Don't _____ paper scraps.	win wet waste
2	Take an old picture _____.	frame from farm
3	_____ scraps onto it.	Pass Pat Paste
4	Draw your _____.	face fan fin
5	_____ it in the frame.	Tap Tape Tip
6	Hang it in a good _____.	place pal plate

Recycle Today

How can you stop waste today?
Tate and Miss Jay have a way.

They say, "Save your lunch trays.
Don't toss them away.

Use them when you work
Or when you play.

Or use them to make gifts
For your friend's birthday!"

1. We need to stop _____.

2. Tate and Miss Jay save lunch _____.

3. They use them when they _____.

4. Use a tray to make a _____ gift.

Use the picture clues to fill in the puzzles.
Print one letter in each box.

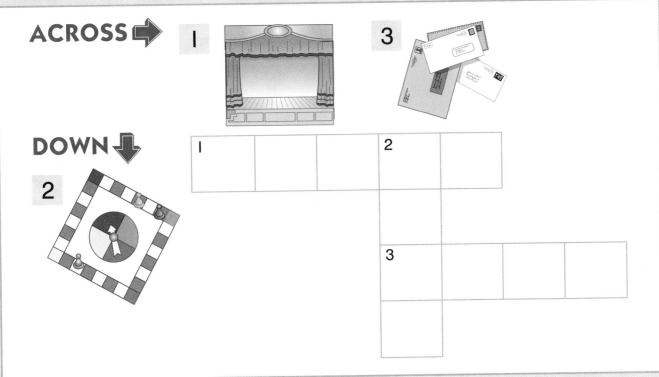

ACROSS ➡ 1   3

DOWN ⬇

2

ACROSS ➡ 1   2

DOWN ⬇

1

LESSON 78: Reviewing Long Vowel **a**   **159**

Unscramble the words to make a sentence. Write the sentence on the line. Then circle the long **a** words.

1   is   big   This   day.   the

_____

2   waves.   Jake   hear   can

_____

3   waits   He   the   bay.   by

_____

4   way.   is   the   Dave   on

_____

5   Dave   bait.   the   has

_____

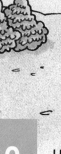

LESSON 78: Reviewing Long Vowel **a**

Read the poem together. Draw a line under the long **i** words. Then color the **hive, pine, vine,** and **five** bees.

Five in the Hive

Five bees wake up.
They leave the **hive**.
They see a **vine**,
And down they **dive**.

I **like** bees.
They're very **wise**.
Bees do **fine** work
For their small **size**.

1	2	3	4
5	6	7	8
9	10	11	12
13	14	15	16

Say the name of each picture. Circle the pictures whose names rhyme. Then make a new rhyming word.

1	5			___ive
2			6	___ide
3				___ire
4			_____	___ine

h	br	sm
f d	s k	p t
p n v	h r t	m j f

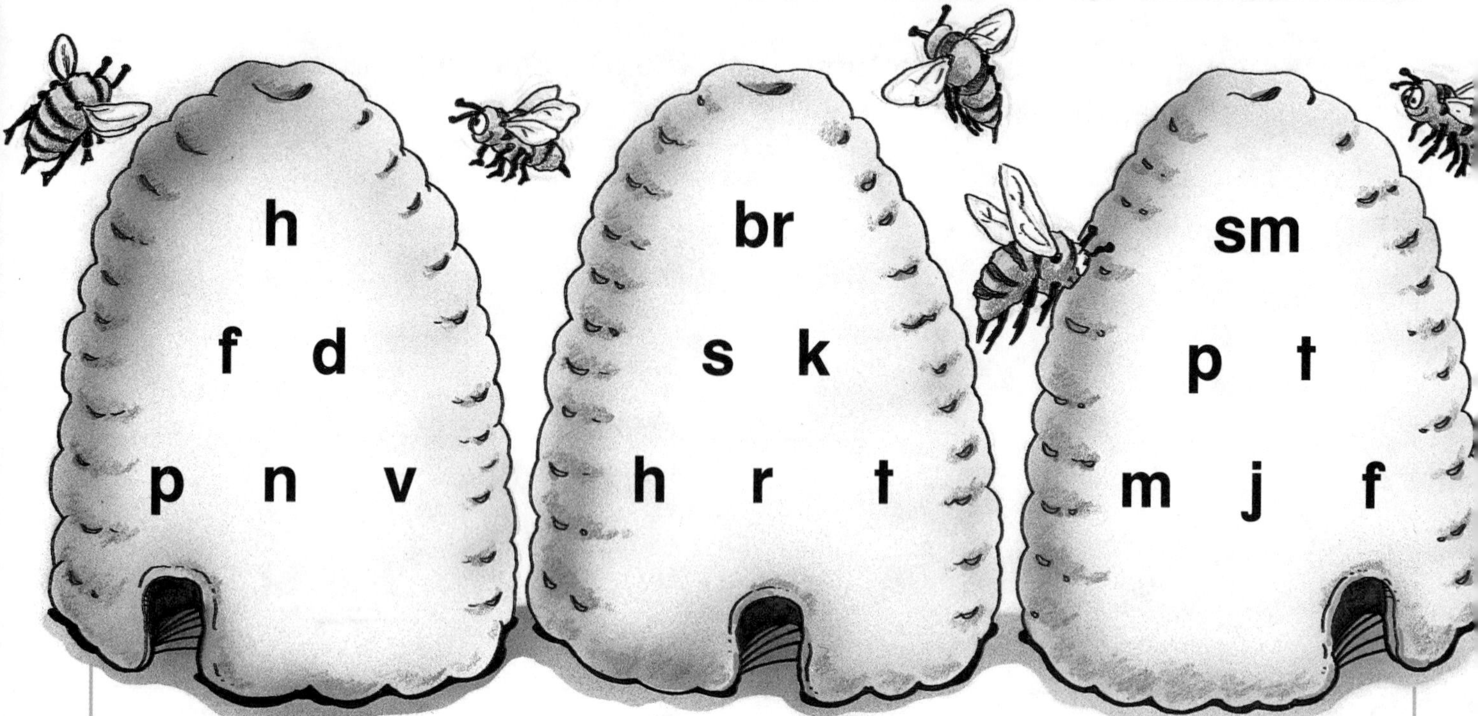

_ine

_ide

_ile

fine

LESSON 80: Long Vowel **i** Phonograms

Circle the word that names each picture.

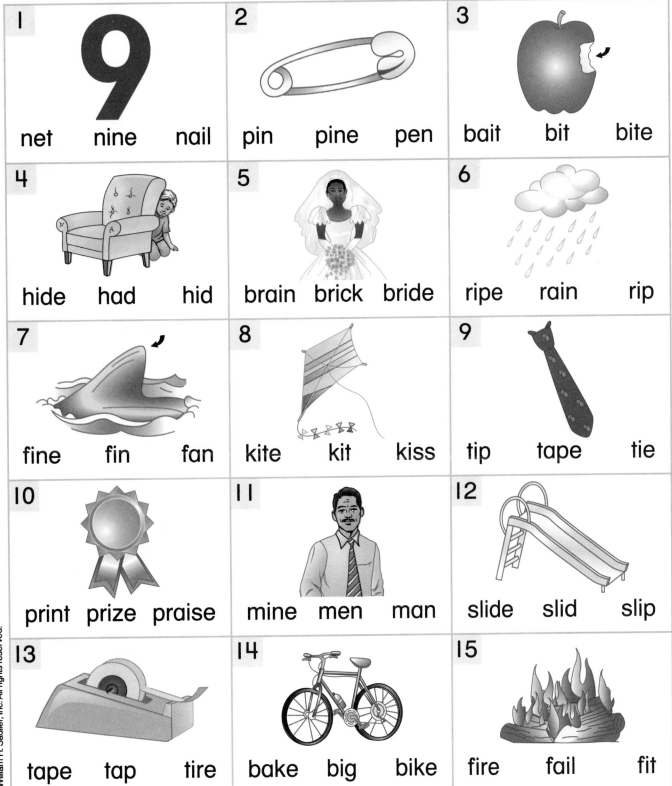

1 net nine nail	**2** pin pine pen	**3** bait bit bite
4 hide had hid	**5** brain brick bride	**6** ripe rain rip
7 fine fin fan	**8** kite kit kiss	**9** tip tape tie
10 print prize praise	**11** mine men man	**12** slide slid slip
13 tape tap tire	**14** bake big bike	**15** fire fail fit

1
land
line
lips

_____

2
dime
dim
damp

3
6
sax
six
side

4
5
fake
fix
five

5
hit
hot
hide

6
dice
day
date

7
pit
pie
pay

8
time
tab
tub

9
pain
pin
pine

10
ride
rip
rail

11
rake
rice
ring

12
van
vine
vest

Say the name of each picture. Print it on the line.

1	2	3	4

5	6	7	8

9	10

11	12

5

Say the name of each picture. If the name has the sound of long **i,** write it on the long **i** bin. Then, if the name has the sound of short **i,** write it on the short **i** bin.

Long **i**

Short **i**

LESSON 82: Discriminating Between Long **i** and Short **i**

Look at the picture. Circle the word that completes the sentence. Print it on the line.

#	Picture	Sentence	Words
1		It is a _____ day.	fine / fin / fail
2		We _____ to Pine Lake.	ride / red / rake
3	PINE LAKE	It is just one _____ .	mail / mall / mile
4		We _____ and swim.	hill / hike / have
5		Mom makes a _____ .	fan / fill / fire
6		What a _____ day!	nest / name / nice

I Like the Earth

I like the earth.
I like tall pines,
And buds that smile
On leafy vines,
And fine, clear lakes
Where I can dive,
And bees that buzz
Inside their hive.

1. Tall _____ are nice.

2. Buds can grow on _____.

3. It's fun to _____ in lakes.

4. Bees buzz inside a _____.

Print **a** or **i** in each empty box to make two words.
Read the words across and down.

1

```
      h
t  i  d  e
      d
      e
```

2

```
      g
t     m  e
      m
      e
```

3

```
      p
c     g  e
      g
      e
```

4

```
      b
k     t  e
      t
      e
```

5

```
      h
b     k  e
      k
      e
```

6

```
      s
p     i  l
      i
      l
```

Look at each picture and read the sentences. Fill in the circle before the sentence that tells about the picture.

1.
○ Tasha drives the bus.

○ Tasha rides her bike.

2.
○ Rafe plants a pine.

○ Rafe likes the hive.

3.
○ Lee drops the can in the lake.

○ Lee takes the cans to the bin.

4.
○ Ike will toss the scraps away.

○ Ike lets the pigs eat from the pail.

5.
○ Mike takes a hike with Dad.

○ Mike asks Dad for a ride.

6.
○ Kate bakes a pie.

○ Kate makes a kite.

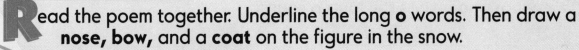

Read the poem together. Underline the long **o** words. Then draw a **nose, bow,** and a **coat** on the figure in the snow.

Let It Snow

I grab my **coat**
And out I **go**
To make **snow** people
In the **snow**.

I'll **coast** down hills,
And make a fort.
A **snowy** day
Is much too short!

Snow has the long **o** sound. Circle and color each picture whose name has the long **o** sound.

O

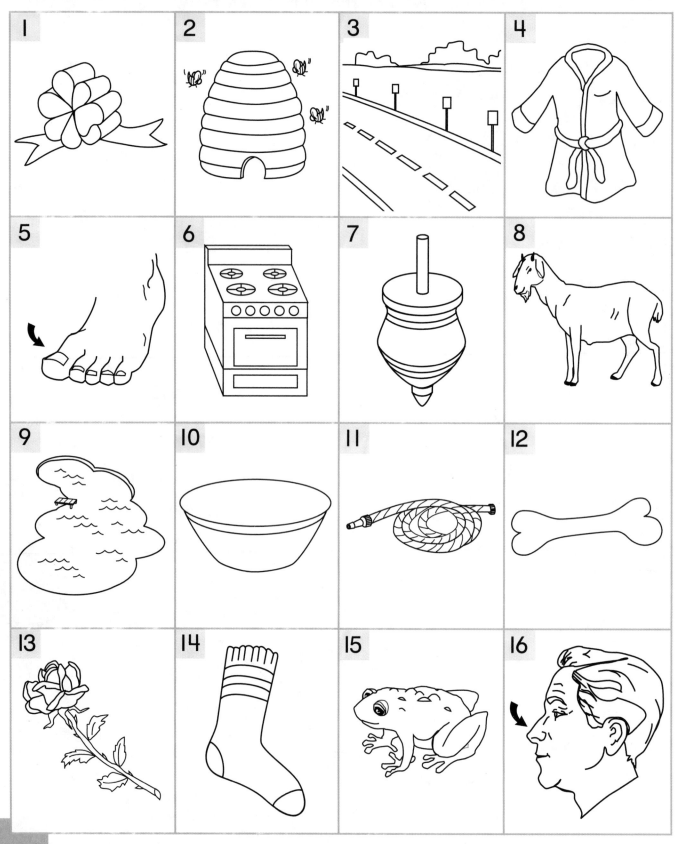

Help Joe recycle. Say the name of the picture on each newspaper. Color the newspapers with rhyming words the same color.

1

2

3

4

5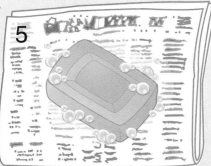

6

7

8

9

10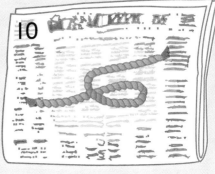

11

12

Say the name of each picture. Circle the pictures whose names rhyme. Then make a new rhyming word.

1. ___ow

2. ___ose

3. ___one

4. ___oat

LESSON 86: Long Vowel **o** Phonograms

Say each word ending. Say the name of each picture. Print the word on the line. Then add your own rhyming word and picture.

_ose	_oat	_ow
1	4	7
2	5	8
3	6	9

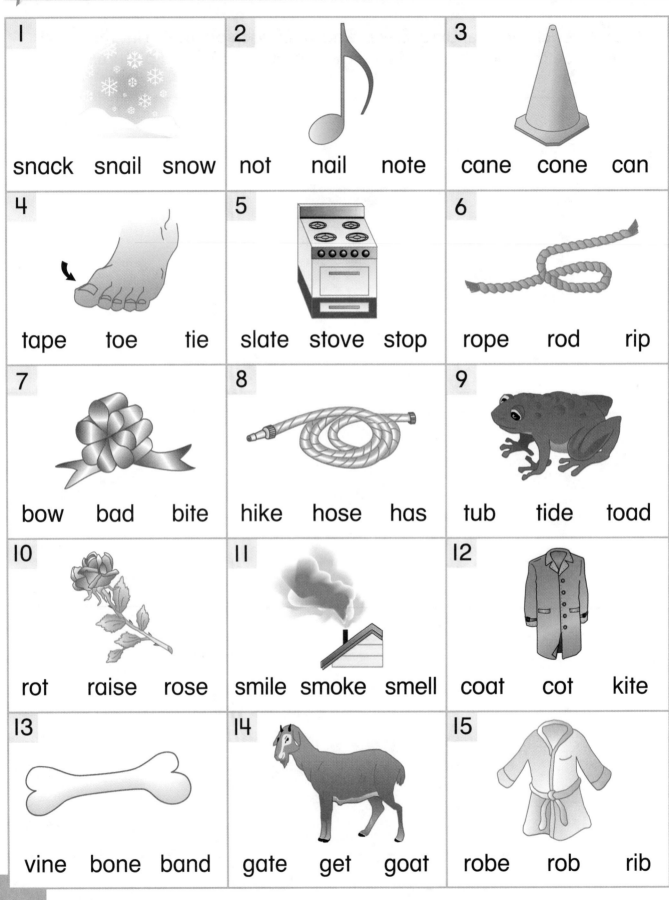

1. snack   snail   snow

2. not   nail   note

3. cane   cone   can

4. tape   toe   tie

5. slate   stove   stop

6. rope   rod   rip

7. bow   bad   bite

8. hike   hose   has

9. tub   tide   toad

10. rot   raise   rose

11. smile   smoke   smell

12. coat   cot   kite

13. vine   bone   band

14. gate   get   goat

15. robe   rob   rib

ay the name of each picture. Circle the word and print it on the line.

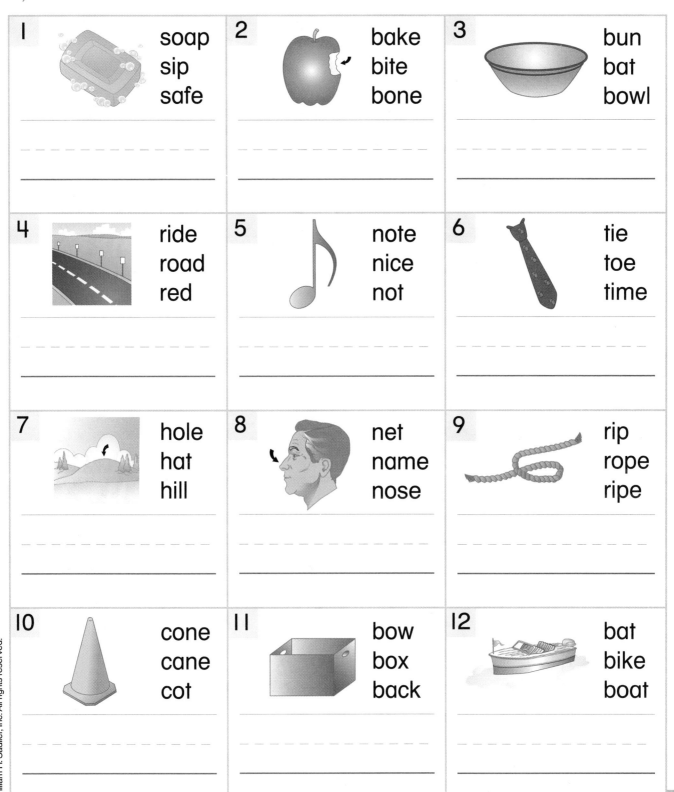

1 soap
sip
safe

_____

2 bake
bite
bone

_____

3 bun
bat
bowl

_____

4 ride
road
red

_____

5 note
nice
not

_____

6 tie
toe
time

_____

7 hole
hat
hill

_____

8 net
name
nose

_____

9 rip
rope
ripe

_____

10 cone
cane
cot

_____

11 bow
box
back

_____

12 bat
bike
boat

_____

Lesson 88: Practicing Long Vowel o

179

Read the name of each picture. Circle **L** if the name has the sound of long **o**. Circle **S** if the name has the sound of short **o**. Then color the pictures whose names have the sound of long **o**.

1	2	3	4
block	goat	bone	fox
L S	L S	L S	L S

5	6	7	8
pop	boat	rose	log
L S	L S	L S	L S

9	10	11	12
cone	snow	box	mop
L S	L S	L S	L S

13	14	15	16
dog	rock	bow	toe
L S	L S	L S	L S

Look at each picture. Circle the word that completes the sentence. Print it on the line.

1 Look at the _____.

snip
snake
snow

2 It is _____ white at first.

so
say
sock

3 There is dirt on the _____.

rope
rake
road

4 It is from _____.

smile
smoke
smell

5 Snow _____ up dirt.

soaps
soaks
sacks

6 Our _____ do, too!

cots
cast
coats

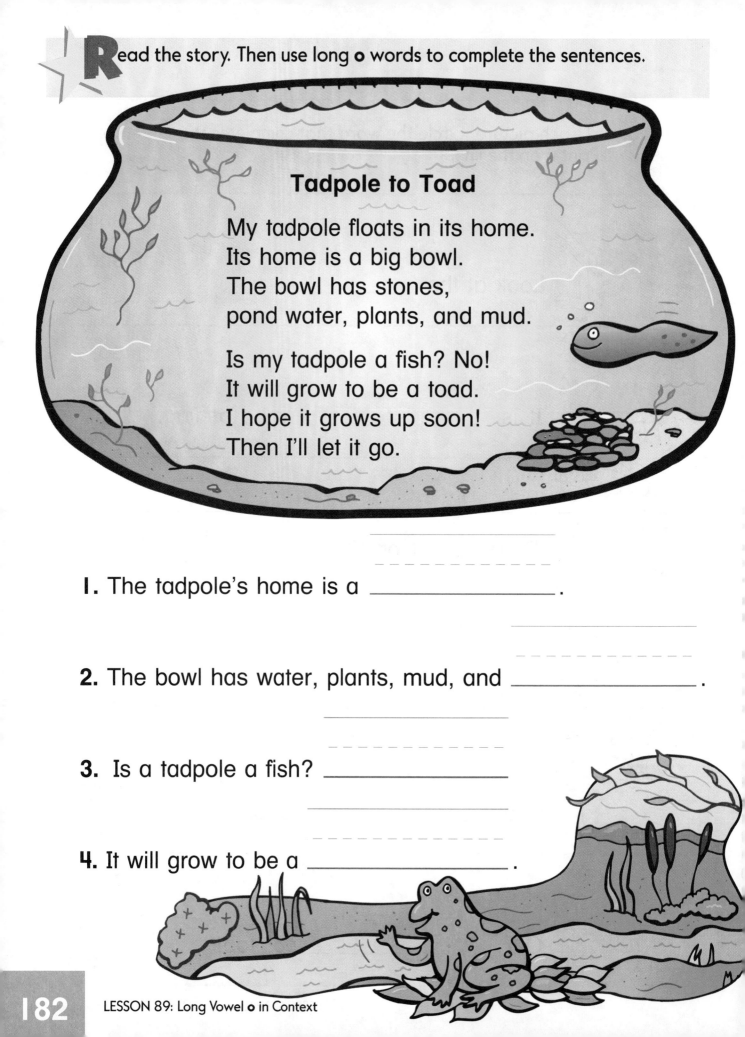

Tadpole to Toad

My tadpole floats in its home.
Its home is a big bowl.
The bowl has stones,
pond water, plants, and mud.

Is my tadpole a fish? No!
It will grow to be a toad.
I hope it grows up soon!
Then I'll let it go.

1. The tadpole's home is a _____.

2. The bowl has water, plants, mud, and _____.

3. Is a tadpole a fish? _____

4. It will grow to be a _____.

Read the words in the boxes. Combine words from boxes 1, 2, and 3 to make sentences. Print them on the lines. Then go back and underline the long vowel words in the sentences.

1	2	3
Kate and Jane	ride	to the lake.
Joe and Joan	race	down the road.
Five men	will go	to the pines.

1
- ○ tip
- ○ tape
- ○ tap

2
- ○ bit
- ○ bite
- ○ boat

3
- ○ vine
- ○ vane
- ○ van

4
- ○ pain
- ○ pin
- ○ pine

5
- ○ cane
- ○ cone
- ○ kite

6
- ○ ride
- ○ robe
- ○ rid

7
- ○ soap
- ○ side
- ○ sail

8
- ○ slide
- ○ slid
- ○ slate

9
- ○ pal
- ○ pole
- ○ pail

10
- ○ cot
- ○ cat
- ○ coat

11
- ○ goat
- ○ gate
- ○ get

12
- ○ hide
- ○ hot
- ○ had

13
- ○ ran
- ○ rain
- ○ rose

14
- ○ robe
- ○ rob
- ○ ripe

15
- ○ nine
- ○ not
- ○ note

Read the poem together. Underline the long **u** words. Then color the sand **dunes**, bathing **suits**, inner **tubes**, and **fruit**. Color the sky **blue**.

It's June

Blue skies,
Bathing **suit**,
Inner **tubes**,
Fresh **fruit**,

Sandy **dunes**,
Happy **tunes**,
Hurray, no **school**,
Yes, it's **June**.

u

 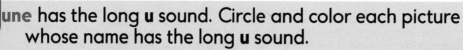**J**une has the long **u** sound. Circle and color each picture whose name has the long **u** sound.

LESSON 91: Recognizing the Sound of Long Vowel **u**

Look at the calendar page. Find and color the pictures with long **u** in their names: **cubes, flute, fruit, juice, mule, tuba**.

In each row, circle the word that rhymes with the name of the picture in the box.

#	Picture			
1	**fl**ute	cute	cut	cane
2	**c**ube	tape	tub	tube
3	**d**une	tone	tune	time
4	**fr**uit	suit	size	sun
5	**m**ule	rail	rule	run
6	**gl**ue	plum	cub	blue

LESSON 92: Long Vowel **u** in Rhyming Words

Say each word ending. Say the name of each picture. Print the word on the line. Then add your own rhyming words.

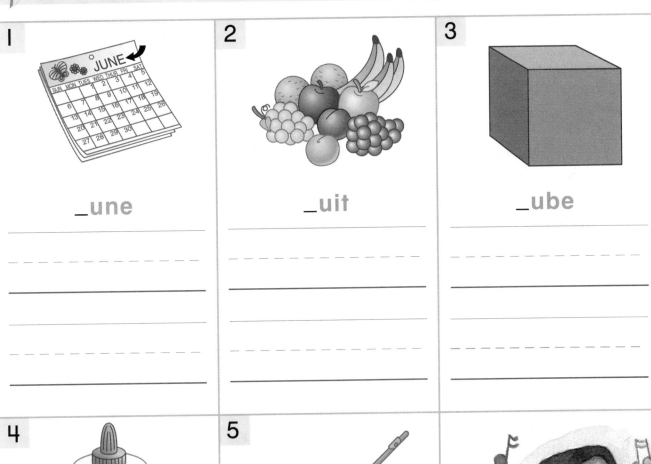

1

_une

_____

- - - - - - - - - - - - -

_____

_____

2

_uit

_____

- - - - - - - - - - - - -

_____

_____

3

_ube

_____

- - - - - - - - - - - - -

_____

_____

4

_ue

_____

- - - - - - - - - - - - -

_____

_____

5

_ute

_____

- - - - - - - - - - - - -

_____

_____

LESSON 93: Practicing Long Vowel **u** Phonograms

189

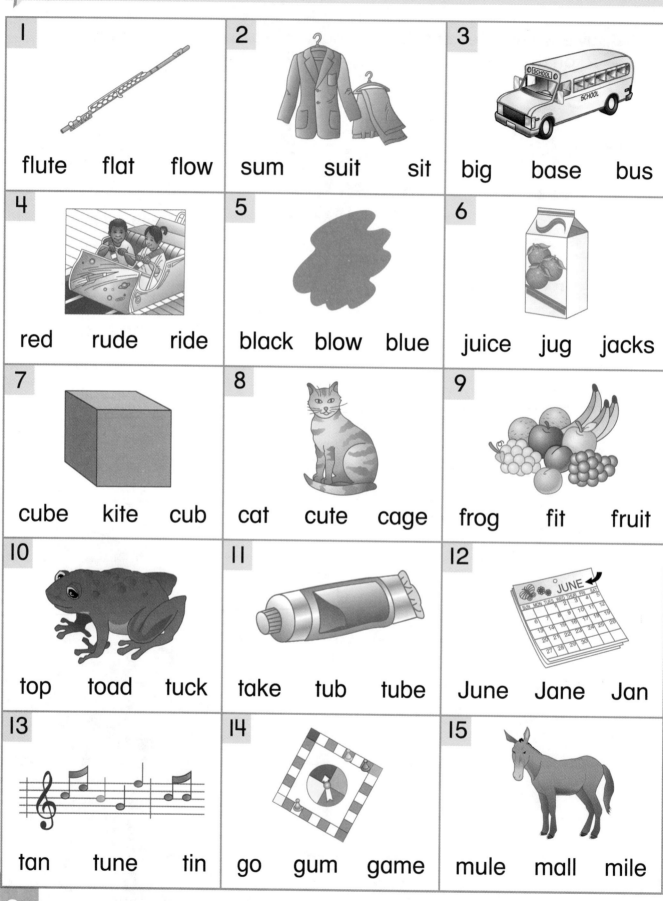

1

flute   flat   flow

2

sum   suit   sit

3

big   base   bus

4

red   rude   ride

5

black   blow   blue

6

juice   jug   jacks

7

cube   kite   cub

8

cat   cute   cage

9

frog   fit   fruit

10

top   toad   tuck

11

take   tub   tube

12

June   Jane   Jan

13

tan   tune   tin

14

go   gum   game

15

mule   mall   mile

Say the name of each picture. Print it on the line. In the last box, draw a picture of a long **u** word. Print the word on the line.

1	2	3
4	5	6
7	8	9
10	11	12

Say the name of each picture. If the name has the sound of long **u**, write it under the long **u** tube. If the name has the sound of short **u**, write it under the short **u** tube.

Long **u**

Short **u**

LESSON 94: Discriminating Between Long **u** and Short **u**

Look at each picture. Circle the word that completes the sentence. Print it on the line.

1	Sue will make a _____ .	fun / flute / flat
2	She uses a _____ .	tub / tape / tube
3	She will paint it _____ .	blow / blue / bug
4	Luke brings his _____ .	tuba / tag / tug
5	Julia will _____ an old box.	use / us / as
6	They will play a _____ .	toad / tan / tune

What Am I?

I have blue skies,
great seas,
lively beasts,
ripe fruit,
soft winds that sound
like flutes
and beauty everywhere.

Rude people pollute me.
My true friends salute me.
What am I?

Did you guess the earth?

1. The skies are _____.

2. The _____ is ripe.

3. _____ people pollute me.

4. Winds sound like _____.

Read the cartoon about Luke. Draw a line under the long **u** words.

1. Luke is not rude.

2. He takes Mom some juice.

3. Then he fills the ice cube tray.

4. He gets a seat for Aunt June.

5. He uses a napkin.

6. Luke is a true pal.

LESSON 96: Reading Long Vowel **u**

195

Use a long **u** word to complete each good manners rule. The words in the box will help you.

juice	rude	cube	Use

Use Good Manners

1. Try not to be _____.

2. Wipe up spilled _____.

3. Fill the ice _____ tray.

4. _____ a napkin at dinner.

5. Write a sentence to tell how you use good manners.

_____

_____

Say the name of each picture. Then find the name in the puzzle and circle it. Color the picture after you circle its name.

U C U B E
N O T E M
T A I L U
D T R X L
P I E Z E

Unscramble the words to make a sentence. Write the sentence on the line. Then go back and circle the long vowel words.

1   June.   in   nice   is   earth   The

_____

_____

2   in   pines.   the   Jays   play

_____

_____

3   blue.   sky   so   is   The

_____

_____

4   We   outside.   play   can

_____

_____

5   coats   away.   our   We   put

_____

_____

6   ride   We   bikes   day.   all

_____

_____

Read the poem together. Draw a line under the long **e** words. Complete the picture by drawing a person or animal.

Green Trees

Green trees,
Green trees!
They give us wood
And things to **eat.**
Branches hold
Our swing's **seat.**
We think **trees**
Are really **neat!**

Tree has the long **e** sound. Circle and color each picture whose name has the long **e** sound.

e

LESSON 98: Recognizing the Sound of Long Vowel **e**

Find each pair of pictures with rhyming names.
Color their leaves the same color.

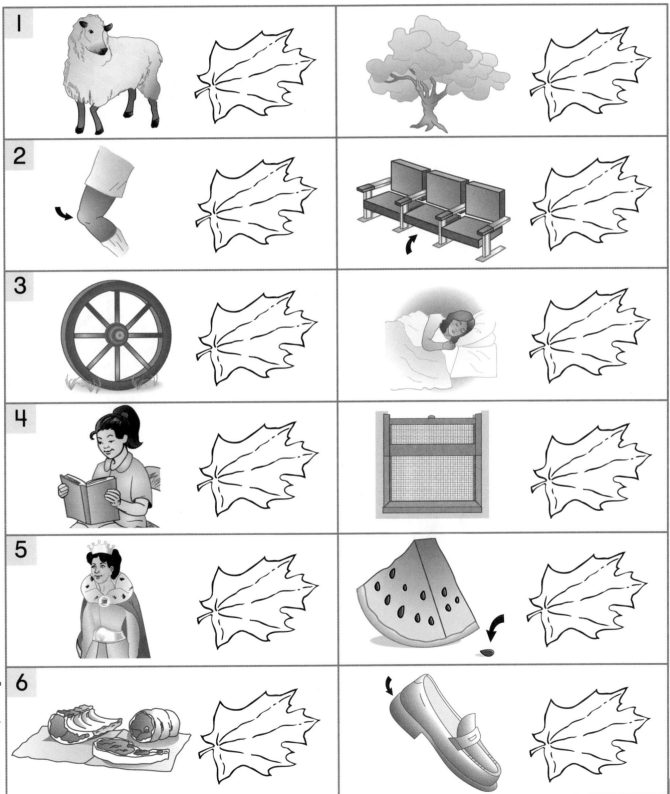

Say each word ending. Say the name of each picture. Print the word on the line. Then add your own rhyming word and picture.

_ee	_eel	_eep
1	4	7
2	5	8
3	6	9

LESSON 99: Long Vowel **e** Phonograms

Add the beginning sound on each petal to the word part on the flower pot below it. Write the new words on the lines.

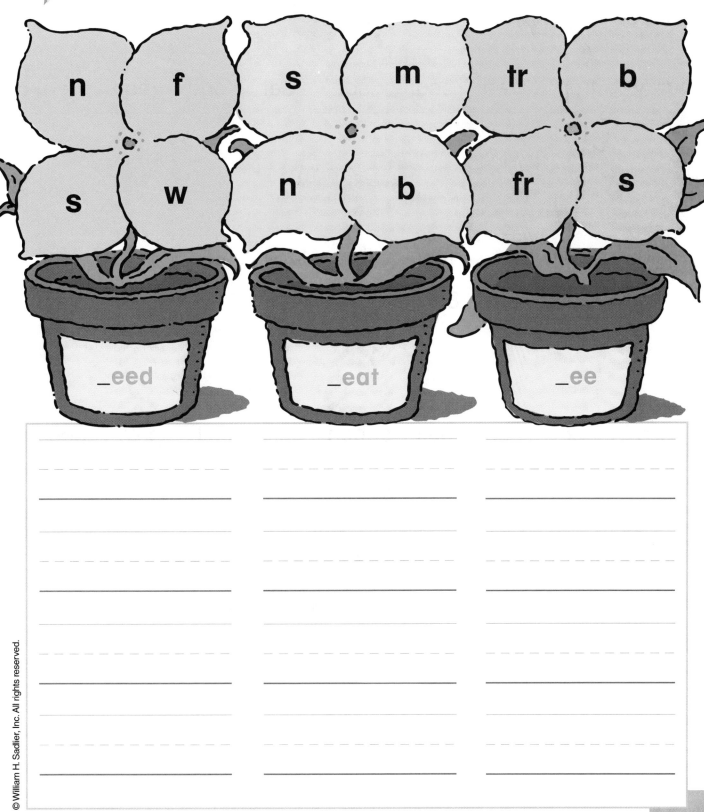

| n | f | s | m | tr | b |
| s | w | n | b | fr | s |

_eed   _eat   _ee

Circle the word that names each picture.

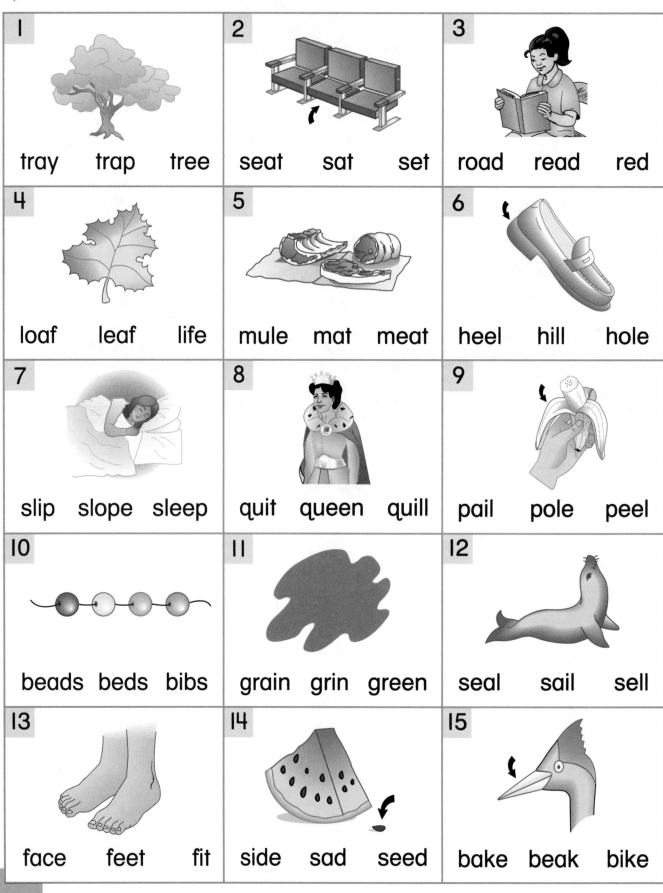

1	2	3
tray trap tree	seat sat set	road read red

4	5	6
loaf leaf life	mule mat meat	heel hill hole

7	8	9
slip slope sleep	quit queen quill	pail pole peel

10	11	12
beads beds bibs	grain grin green	seal sail sell

13	14	15
face feet fit	side sad seed	bake beak bike

Say the name of each picture. Circle the word and print it on the line.

1 eat / egg / it	2 jet / jump / jeep	3 sale / seal / sell
4 tame / time / team	5 bow / bee / bay	6 mule / mitt / meat
7 true / trip / tree	8 read / ride / rude	9 pal / peel / pile
10 sit / seat / suit	11 peas / pies / pays	12 left / let / leaf

Read the name of each picture. Circle **L** if the name has the sound of long **e**. Circle **S** if the name has the sound of short **e**. Then color the pictures whose names have the sound of long **e**.

1	2	3	4
beads	bed	ten	meat
L S	L S	L S	L S

5	6	7	8
seed	beg	men	peas
L S	L S	L S	L S

9	10	11	12
desk	pet	beak	read
L S	L S	L S	L S

13	14	15	16
team	bee	sled	hen
L S	L S	L S	L S

LESSON 101: Discriminating Between Long **e** and Short **e**

Look at the picture. Circle the word that completes the sentence. Print it on the line.

1. Dee put on her _____.

   jets
   jacks
   jeans

2. Now she _____ a bag.

   needs
   nods
   nails

3. She will _____ Uncle Pete.

   mat
   meet
   mitt

4. They will go to the _____.

   buck
   back
   beach

5. Each _____ they meet there.

   week
   wet
   wake

6. They _____ up the beach.

   clip
   clay
   clean

In the Big Tree

Last week Dad and I
saw a big tree.
Dad said, "Stay still, Lee.
Hear the baby birds peep."

I looked up and saw
three baby birds in a nest.
Dad said, "Their mother will bring
some things to feed them."

1. Last _____ we saw a big tree.

2. We could _____ the baby birds.

3. _____ baby birds were in a nest.

4. Their mother will _____ them.

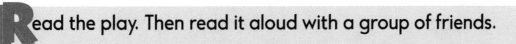
We Need Each Other

 I am a tree. People need me.
I give them wood and sweet fruit to eat.

 We need trees!

 I am the deep sea. People need me.
I am a place for fish to swim free.

 We need the sea!

 I am a bee. People need me.
I speed from bud to bud and help flowers grow.

 We need bees!

 And we need people, too!
We need people to take care of the earth.
We need people to help all living things.

Look at each picture below. Write what the Clean Team is doing. The words in the box may help you.

clean	sweep	team	seed	weed	seen
keep	green	need	tree	eat	need

Use the picture clues to fill in the puzzle. Then use the letters in the boxes to finish the message in the sand.

1. ¹K i t e

2. __ ² __

3. __ __ __ ³

4. __ __ __ ⁴

5. ⁵ __ __ __

6. ⁶ __ __ __

7. __ __ __ ⁷

K __ __ __ __ __ __   beach clean.
1   2   3   4   5   6   7

Read the sentences. First number the sentences in order to tell a story. Then print the sentences in order on the lines.

_____ Then she gave it water.

_____ Next she put the pine tree in it.

_____ Now she waits for it to grow.

_____ First June made a hole.

1. _____

2. _____

3. _____

4. _____

When **y** is at the end of a word, it can have the sound of long **i**, as in **sky**, or the sound of long **e**, as in **bunny**.

Say the name of each picture. If the **y** at the end of the word has the long **i** sound, circle the picture. If the **y** at the end of the word has the long **e** sound, draw a line under the picture.

 sky

 bunny

LESSON 105: Recognizing Final **y** as a Vowel

213

Say the name of each picture. Circle the word and print it on the line.

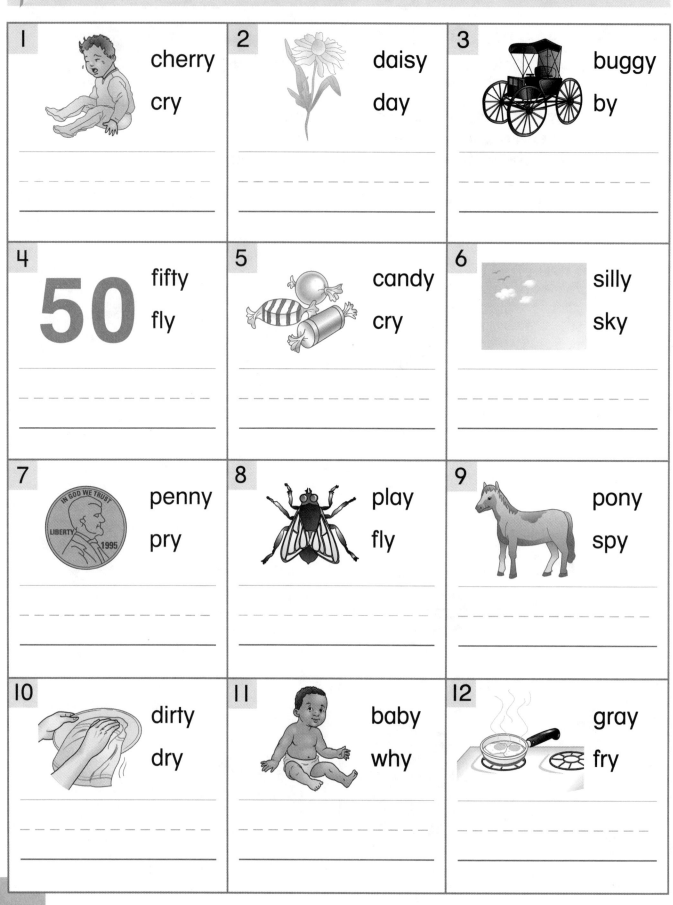

1. cherry
   cry
   _____

2. daisy
   day
   _____

3. buggy
   by
   _____

4. **50** fifty
   fly
   _____

5. candy
   cry
   _____

6. silly
   sky
   _____

7. penny
   pry
   _____

8. play
   fly
   _____

9. pony
   spy
   _____

10. dirty
    dry
    _____

11. baby
    why
    _____

12. gray
    fry
    _____

Read the name of each picture. Circle **i** if the **y** in the name has the sound of long **i**. Circle **e** if the **y** in the name has the sound of long **e**.

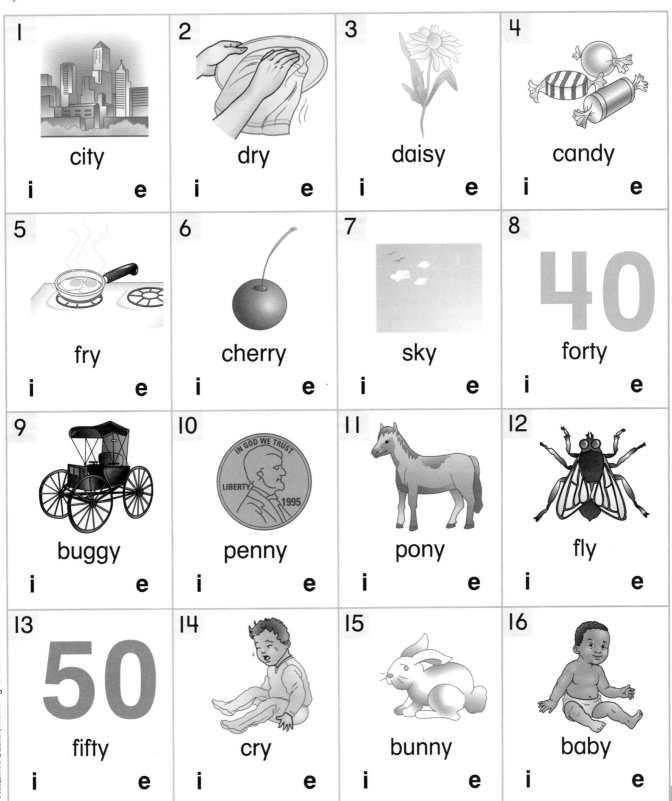

1 city — i e	2 dry — i e	3 daisy — i e	4 candy — i e
5 fry — i e	6 cherry — i e	7 sky — i e	8 forty — i e
9 buggy — i e	10 penny — i e	11 pony — i e	12 fly — i e
13 fifty — i e	14 cry — i e	15 bunny — i e	16 baby — i e

LESSON 106: Discriminating Between Final **y** as Long **e** and Long **i**

215

fuzzy	sky	happy	windy	cry	baby

1. It was _____ outside.

2. But the _____ was sunny and blue.

3. Billy's baby sister started to _____ .

4. Billy put the _____ in the buggy.

5. He put the _____ bear in, too.

6. They were _____ to be outside.

Spell and Write Say and spell the words in the box. Then print each word under the vowel sound in its name.

bike
use
gave
hose
jay
juice
keep
like
own
seed
bunny
sky

Long a
1 gave
2

Long o
7
8

Long i
3
4

Long e
9
10

Long u
5
6

y as Long i
11

y as Long e
12

Spell and Write Pretend that you are in the picture. Write what you would say to Jake and Lane to tell them how they can be kind to the earth. Use one or more of your spelling words.

bike	gave	jay	keep	own	like
use	hose	juice	bunny	seed	sky

To Jake: _____

_____

_____

_____

_____

To Lane: _____

_____

_____

_____

RECYCLE

Check-Up Fill in the circle next to the name of each picture.

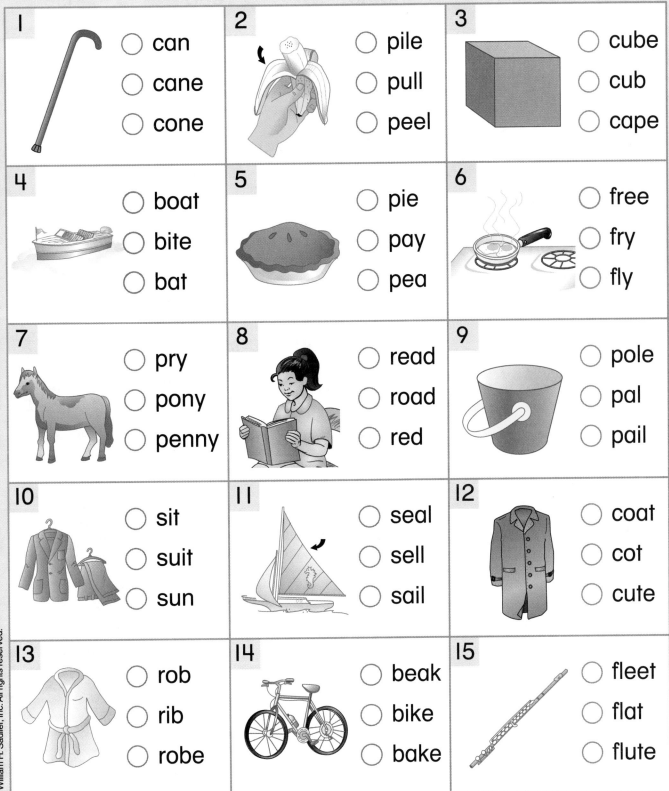

1.
- ○ can
- ○ cane
- ○ cone

2.
- ○ pile
- ○ pull
- ○ peel

3.
- ○ cube
- ○ cub
- ○ cape

4.
- ○ boat
- ○ bite
- ○ bat

5.
- ○ pie
- ○ pay
- ○ pea

6.
- ○ free
- ○ fry
- ○ fly

7.
- ○ pry
- ○ pony
- ○ penny

8.
- ○ read
- ○ road
- ○ red

9.
- ○ pole
- ○ pal
- ○ pail

10.
- ○ sit
- ○ suit
- ○ sun

11.
- ○ seal
- ○ sell
- ○ sail

12.
- ○ coat
- ○ cot
- ○ cute

13.
- ○ rob
- ○ rib
- ○ robe

14.
- ○ beak
- ○ bike
- ○ bake

15.
- ○ fleet
- ○ flat
- ○ flute

Check-Up Use a word from the box to complete each sentence.
Print the word on the line.

bike	tubes	save	pine
seeds	home	read	use

1. You can _____ about helping the earth.

2. Turn off lamps at _____ .

3. Ride your _____ to save gas.

4. Always _____ cans and glass.

5. Try to _____ scraps for art.

6. Make flutes from paper _____ .

7. Plant some _____ .

Say the name of each picture. Circle the word. Then circle **L** if the name has a long vowel sound or **S** if the name has a short vowel sound.

1
cob
cube
cub

L   S

2
bike
bake
beak

L   S

3
mine
mean
men

L   S

4
goat
get
gate

L   S

5
bad
bee
bed

L   S

6
road
rod
read

L   S

7
top
tape
tap

L   S

8
skip
soak
sky

L   S

9
fine
fun
fin

L   S

10
sit
seat
suit

L   S

11
vane
vine
van

L   S

12
mile
mule
meal

L   S

LESSON 109: Reviewing Short and Long Vowels   **221**

A Sale

Jen: My coat is too small, and I can't play the flute.

Tom: We can throw these things away.

Jen: No, let's ask Dad to help us. We can have a sale.

Tom: We can recycle and sell our old things.

Jen: We can use the money to buy seeds to plant.

Tom: The earth will like that! Dad will like that, too!

1. Jen has a small _____.

2. Jen can't play the _____.

3. Tom and Jen will have a _____.

4. They will buy _____ to plant.

Look and Learn

Look at the pictures. Then read and talk about them.

Earth is our home.
Earth gives us nice things
like pine trees, blue lakes,
fruit to eat, and air to breathe.
People must take care of Earth.
We must keep it clean.

How are the people in the
pictures helping Earth?
How can you help Earth?

Check-Up Say the name of each picture. Circle **long** if the name has a long vowel sound or **short** if the name has a short vowel sound. Then print the name of the picture on the line.

1 long short	**2** long short	**3** long short
4 long short	**5** long short	**6** long short
7 long short	**8** long short	**9** long short
10 long short	**11** long short	**12** long short

EARS HEAR

Flies buzz,
Motors roar.
Kettles hiss,
People snore.
Dogs bark,
Birds cheep.
Autos honk: *Beep! Beep!*

Winds sigh,
Shoes squeak,
Trucks honk,
Floors creak.
Whistles toot,
Bells clang.
Doors slam: *Bang! Bang!*

Kids shout,
Clocks ding.
Babies cry,
Phones ring.
Balls bounce,
Spoons drop.
People scream: *Stop! Stop!*

Lucia and James L. Hymes, Jr.

Critical Thinking
What sounds are loud? soft?
What sounds make you feel happy?

LESSON 111: Introduction to Consonant Blends   **225**

Dear Family,

In this unit about our five senses, your child will learn the sounds of consonant blends. As your child progresses through this unit, you can try these activities together at home.

● Say the name of each picture below with your child. Listen to the sounds of the beginning consonant blends **cl**, **tr**, **st**, and the final blend **nd**.

l blend **l** principio	**r** blend **r** principio	**s** blend **s** principio	final blend final
 **cl**ock	 **tr**uck	 **st**op	 ba**nd**

● Read the poem "Ears Hear" on the reverse side of this page.

● Which of your five senses have you used today? What have you seen or heard? What have you tasted or touched or smelled?

● Find words with consonant blends in the poem, such as **flies**, **snore**, **honk**, **trucks**, **clang**, **clocks**, **cry**, **ring**, **spoons**, **drop**, **scream**, and **stop**.

Apreciada Familia:

En esta unidad se enseñarán los cinco sentidos y los sonidos de dos consonantes juntas. Ustedes pueden hacer estas actividades juntos en la casa.

● Con su niño pronuncien el nombre de los objetos en los cuadros. Escuchen los sonidos de las consonantes al principio de la palabra **cl**, **tr**, **st**, y al final **nd**.

● Lea el poema "Ears Hear" en la página 225.

● Hablen sobre estas preguntas: ¿Cuáles de tus sentidos has usado hoy? ¿Qué has tocado, olido o probado? ¿Qué has visto u oído?

● Encuentren sonidos de dos consonantes juntas en el poema, tales como: **flies**, **snore**, **honk**, **trucks**, **clang**, **clocks**, **cry**, **ring**, **spoons**, **drop**, **scream** y **stop**.

PROJECT

Be very quiet, close your eyes for a short time, and listen carefully. Then make a list of sounds you heard in your home or outside. Also list the things that made the sounds. Circle any consonant blends you use.

PROYECTO

Rápido cierren los ojos por poco tiempo y escuchen con cuidado. Luego hagan una lista de los sonidos que escucharon afuera y en la casa. Hagan una lista de lo que hizo el sonido y encierren en un círculo cuando aparezcan dos consonantes juntas.

Clap begins with an **l** blend. In each row, circle and color the pictures whose names begin with the same **l** blend as the picture in the box.

cl

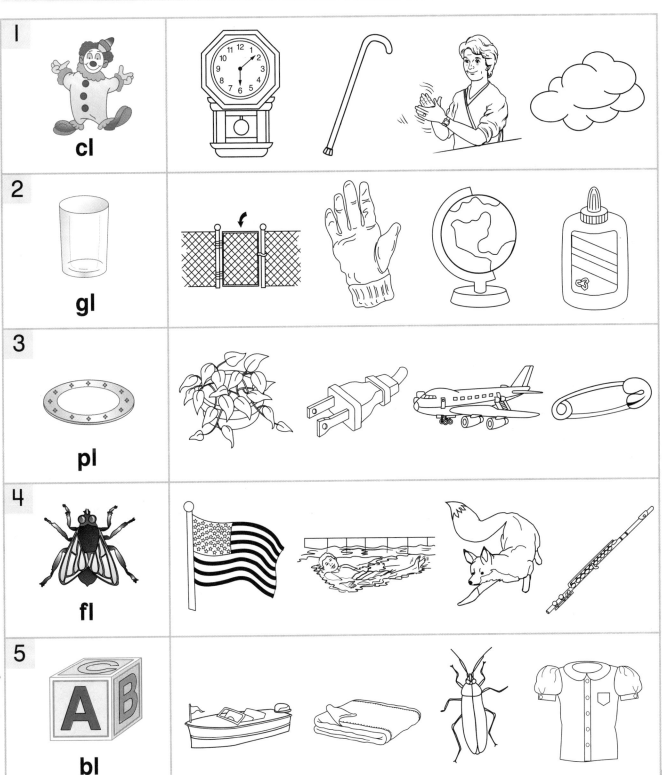

1	**cl**
2	**gl**
3	**pl**
4	**fl**
5	**bl**

LESSON 112: Recognizing **l** Blends

227

Blue, glue, plane, and flag begin with **l** blends. Color the pictures whose names begin with **bl** ▭, **gl** ▭, **pl** ▭, **fl** ▭.

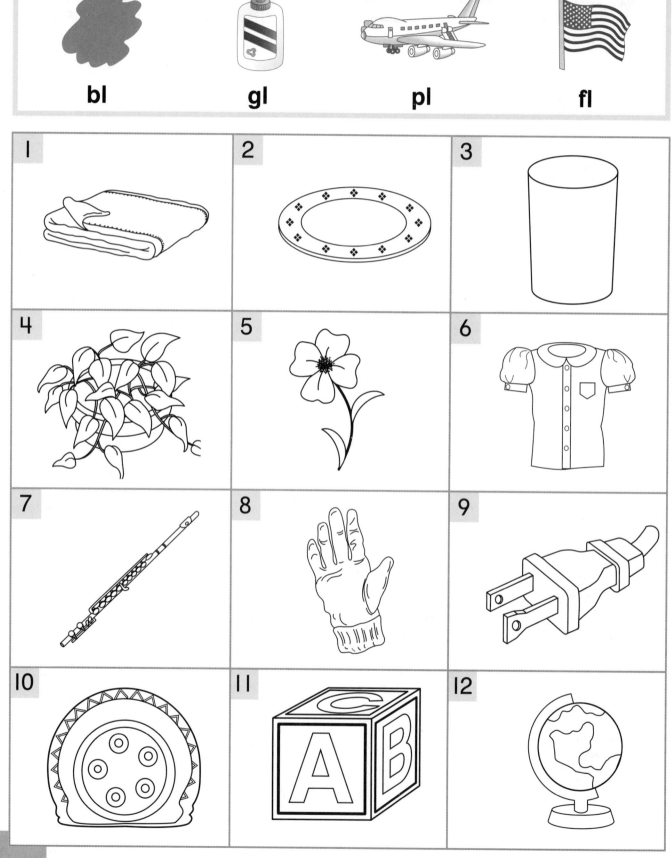

bl　　　**gl**　　　**pl**　　　**fl**

1 flat / fit / feet	**2** bell / bee / blue	**3** cape / clap / cap
4 back / bake / block	**5** pine / plane / pan	**6** flute / fell / fin
7 fry / feel / fly	**8** cake / clock / cot	**9** plug / pig / pry
10 club / cub / cube	**11** late / pat / plate	**12** flag / frog / fig

Read the poem. Then use words from the poem that begin with l blends to complete the sentences.

Our Senses

Hear the wind blow.
See the blue sky.
Hear the clock tick
And the fat, buzzing fly.

Feel the flat glass.
Smell the sweet flower.
Hear the plane roar
As it flies by the tower.

_____

1. I can see the _____ sky.

_____

2. I can hear the _____ buzz.

_____

3. I can feel the flat _____.

_____

4. I can smell a sweet _____.

gr

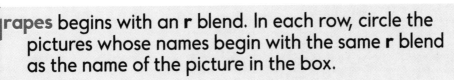
Grapes begins with an **r** blend. In each row, circle the pictures whose names begin with the same **r** blend as the name of the picture in the box.

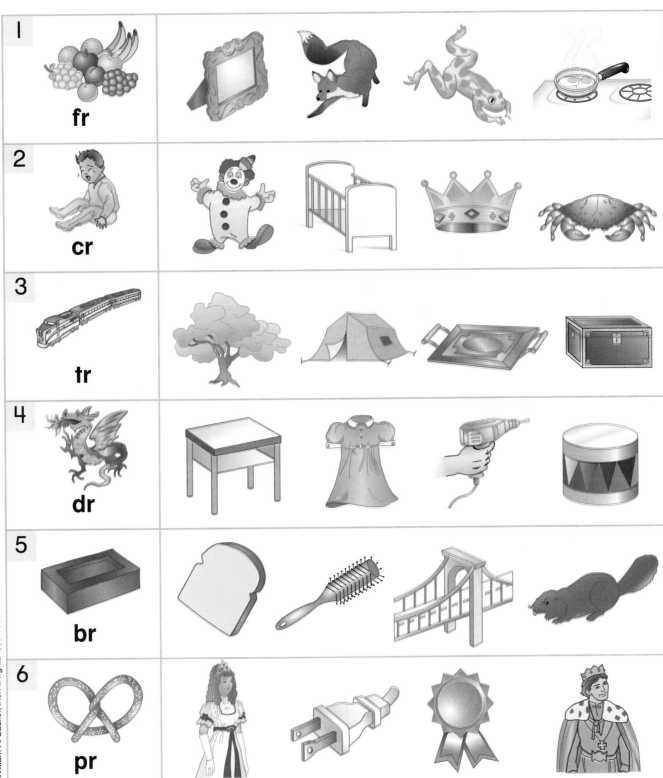

1. **fr**

2. **cr**

3. **tr**

4. **dr**

5. **br**

6. **pr**

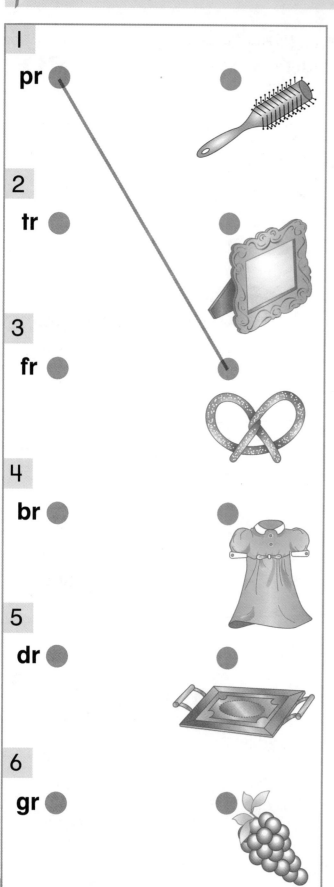

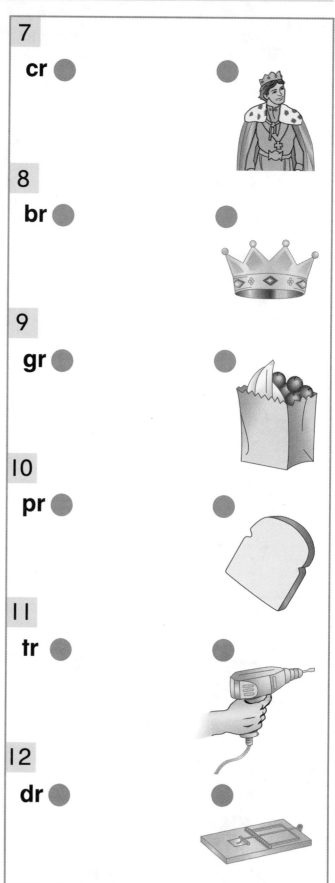

1 **pr**

2 **tr**

3 **fr**

4 **br**

5 **dr**

6 **gr**

7 **cr**

8 **br**

9 **gr**

10 **pr**

11 **tr**

12 **dr**

Say the name of each picture. Circle the name and print it. Then draw a picture of a word that begins with an **r** blend. Print the word.

1	flag fog frog	2	prize plays pies	3	deer drum dime
4	tree tire tie	5	club crab cab	6	fan flame frame
7	bride ride brick	8	globe get green	9	rail drill door
10	cry clay cow	11	rain train tail	12	

© William H. Sadlier, Inc. All rights reserved.

Tasty Treats

I like the taste of bread and jam,
And crispy pretzels, fruit, and ham,
Refried frijoles—tacos, too.
And I love fresh, green grapes, don't you?
And frozen yogurt—what a treat!
It's great to end with something sweet.

1. _____ tastes good with jam.

2. Crispy _____ are good, too.

3. Do you love fresh, green _____?

4. _____ yogurt is a sweet treat.

5. What is your favorite treat? _____

sm

Smell begins with an **s** blend. Say the name of the picture in the middle of each star. Then circle the pictures whose names begin with the same blend.

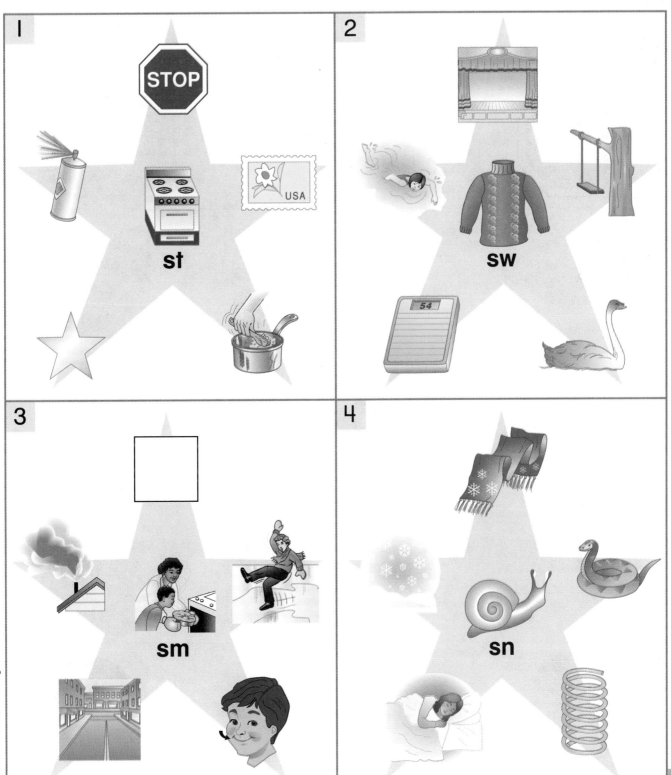

1

STOP

st

2

sw

3

sm

4

sn

Say the name of each picture. Circle the name and print it. Then draw a picture of a word whose name begins with an **s** blend. Print the word.

1 sell / smell / spell	**2** sink / king / skunk	**3** square / star / spare
4 slot / top / stop	**5** spy / say / sky	**6** swell / spill / seal
7 snail / nail / sail	**8** sting / ring / string	**9** slide / side / smile
10 wing / swing / sling	**11** spray / say / ray	**12**

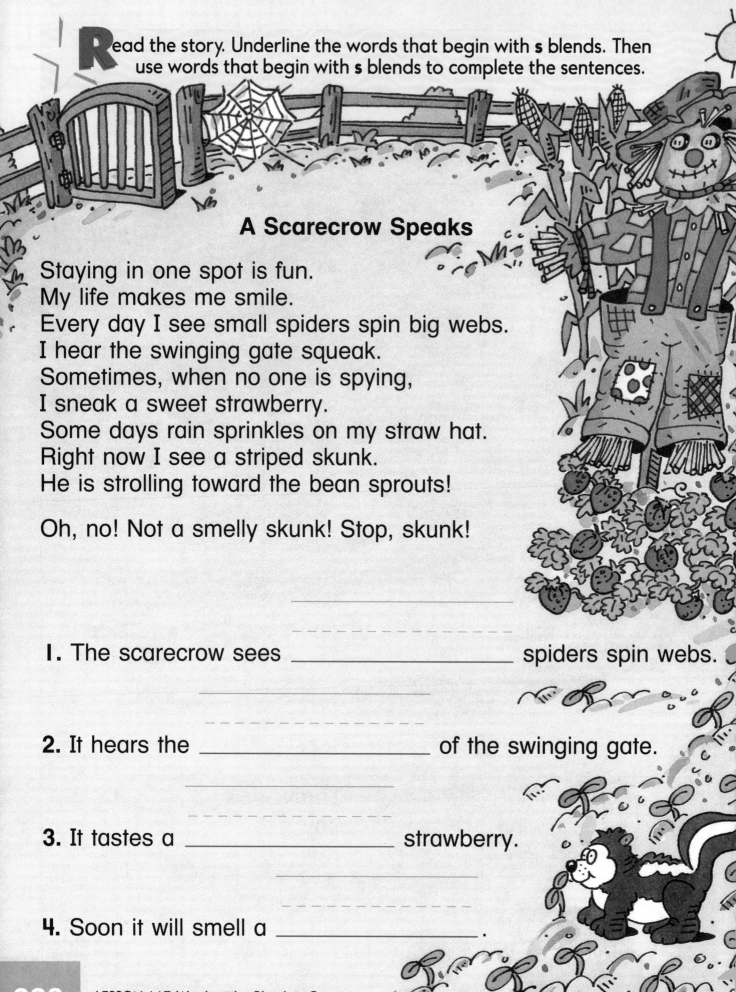

Read the story. Underline the words that begin with **s** blends. Then use words that begin with **s** blends to complete the sentences.

A Scarecrow Speaks

Staying in one spot is fun.
My life makes me smile.
Every day I see small spiders spin big webs.
I hear the swinging gate squeak.
Sometimes, when no one is spying,
I sneak a sweet strawberry.
Some days rain sprinkles on my straw hat.
Right now I see a striped skunk.
He is strolling toward the bean sprouts!

Oh, no! Not a smelly skunk! Stop, skunk!

_____

1. The scarecrow sees _____ spiders spin webs.

2. It hears the _____ of the swinging gate.

3. It tastes a _____ strawberry.

4. Soon it will smell a _____.

Wink ends with the blend **nk**. Other blends, like the ones below can end words, too. Say the name of each picture. Circle the letters that stand for the final blend in each picture's name.

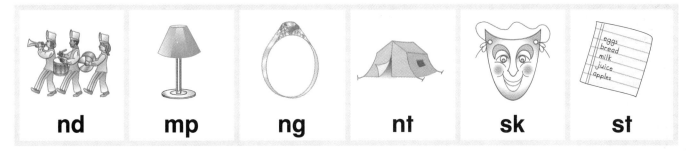

| nd | mp | ng | nt | sk | st |

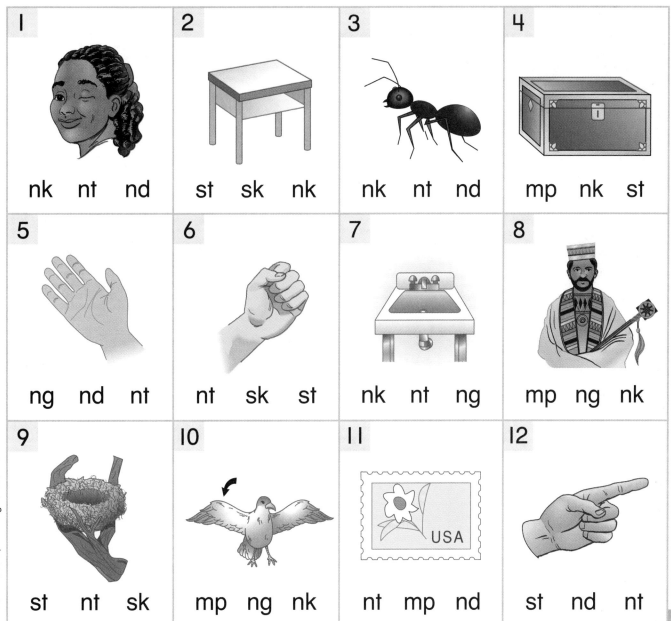

1. nk nt nd

2. st sk nk

3. nk nt nd

4. mp nk st

5. ng nd nt

6. nt sk st

7. nk nt ng

8. mp ng nk

9. st nt sk

10. mp ng nk

11. nt mp nd

12. st nd nt

LESSON 118: Recognizing Final Blends

239

Say the name of each picture. Circle the word and print it on the line.

1	hint had hand	2	kiss king cone	3	desk dime dent
4	win wink wig	5	tent team ten	6	let list lid
7	net note nest	8	mist mask make	9	band bad bat
10	ant ax aim	11	land lime lamp	12	song sink sit

Spell and Write

Say and spell the words in the box. Print each word under the blend in its name. Circle the letters that spell the blends.

small
blue
grill
sweet
dry
glad
long
pretty
band
spin
went
clean

l Blends

1. (bl)ue
2.
3.

s Blends

7.
8.
9.

r Blends

4.
5.
6.

Final Blends

10.
11.
12.

Spell and Write Write a note to thank a friend for a great party. Use some of your spelling words in the note.

| small | grill | dry | long | band | went |
| blue | sweet | glad | pretty | spin | clean |

Dear _____ ,

_____

_____

_____

_____

_____

_____

_____

_____

Your friend,

_____

_____

Use the picture clues to fill in the puzzle.
Print one letter in each box.

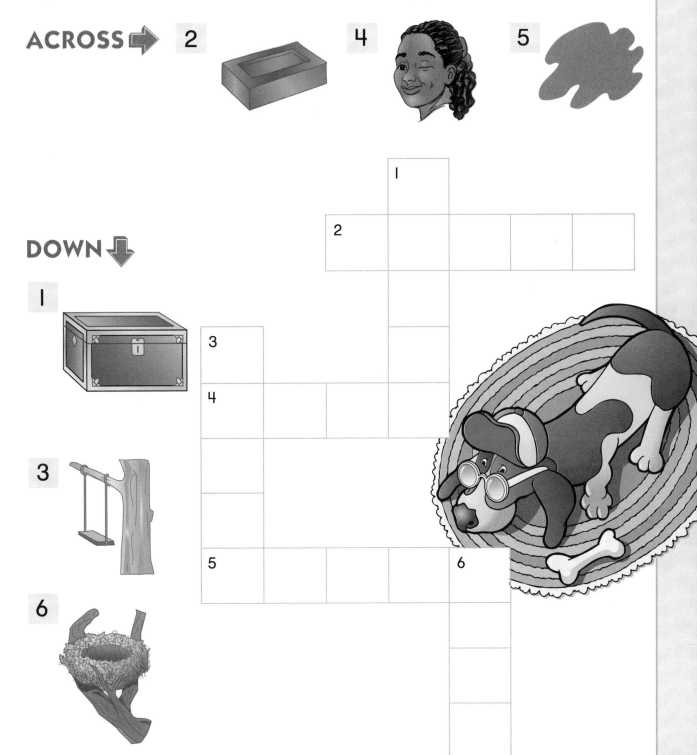

ACROSS ➡ 2   4   5

DOWN ⬇

1

3

6

Read the riddles. Print the answers on the lines.
The picture clues will help you.

1. We like to sing and play.
We make pretty sounds.

_____

We are a _____.

2. We are small black bugs.
We crawl on the ground.

_____

We are _____.

3. I am a blanket of green.
I feel soft when you walk on me.

_____

I am _____.

4. I am black with a white stripe.
People scream when I come near,
but I don't know why.

_____

I am a _____.

5. I am tasty and good to eat.
I am good for you, too.

_____

I am _____.

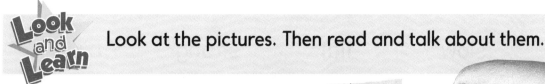

Look at the pictures. Then read and talk about them.

Most people have five senses.
We can see, hear, smell,
taste, and feel. We use our
senses all the time.

Look at the pictures.
Do you see green and blue?
Pretend you are playing the game.
What sound does the crowd make?
Does the mitt feel smooth?
What can you smell?
Wouldn't some crunchy popcorn and
a cool drink taste good right now?

Using all your senses
is fun. Try it!

Think of a thing or animal. Don't tell what it is! Write about it on the lines. Use as many senses as you can to tell about it. Then let a friend guess what it is. The words in the box may help you.

black	slow	flat	strong	blue
dry	lumpy	green	pretty	crisp
long	brown	fresh	rusty	fast

It is a _____.

LESSON 121: Writing Words with Consonant Blends

 **Check-Up** Say the name of each picture. Print the letters that stand for the missing blend on the lines.

1	2	3
___ap	___ane	___ow

4	5	6
ha___	___ee	la___

7	8	9
___ar	de___	___ag

10	11	12
___ide	ne___	___ide

1
○ The dress is green.
○ The dress is blue.

2
○ Miguel plays the flute.
○ The band plays a tune.

3
○ Fran picks up a mask.
○ The fruit tastes sweet.

4
○ Here comes a creepy crab.
○ Here comes a smelly skunk.

5
○ The sink feels soft.
○ The star has a point.

6
○ I hear a plane flying by.
○ I hear the steps squeak.

White sheep, white sheep
On a blue hill,
When the wind stops
You all stand still.
When the wind blows
You walk away slow.
White sheep, white sheep,
Where do you go?

Christina G. Rossetti

Critical Thinking
How would the clouds look on a stormy day?
What do the different kinds of clouds tell you about the weather?

LESSON 123: Introduction to Consonant Digraphs

Dear Family,

In this unit about weather, your child will learn the sounds of consonant digraphs. You can participate with your child by doing these home activities.

● Say the name of each picture below with your child. Listen to the sounds of the beginning consonant digraphs **th**, **sh**, **wh**, **ch**, and **kn**.

Apreciada Familia:

En esta unidad se hablará del tiempo y se enseñarán los sonidos digrafos de las consonantes. Pueden practicarlos con su hijo haciendo estas actividades en la casa.

● Pronuncien el nombre de los objetos en los cuadros. Escuchen los sonidos digrafos de las consonantes al principio de las palabras, **th**, **sh**, **wh**, **ch**, y **kn**.

th	sh	wh	ch	kn
		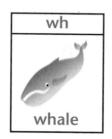	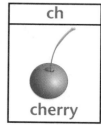	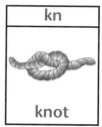
thumb	sheep	whale	cherry	knot

● Read the poem "Clouds" on the reverse side of this page.

● Talk about the shapes of any clouds you can see in the sky. How do they remind you of sheep? What other shapes do you see in the clouds?

● Help your child find words with consonant digraphs in the poem, such as **white**, **sheep**, **when**, and **where**.

● Lean el poema "Clouds" en la página 249.

● Hablen de las diferentes formas de las nubes en el cielo. ¿Te recuerdan a una oveja? ¿Qué otras formas ves?

● Ayuden al niño a encontrar consonantes de sonido digrafo en el poema, tales como: **white**, **sheep**, **when** y **where**.

PROJECT

With your child, read and answer these questions about weather. **Wh**at is the weather like **wh**ere you live? Can you **th**ink of the sound that **th**under makes? Can you find a **sh**adow during a rain **sh**ower? If you had the **ch**ance, how would you **ch**ange the weather?

PROYECTO

Junto con el niño lean y contesten estas preguntas sobre el tiempo. **Wh**at is the weather like **wh**ere you live? Can you **th**ink of the sound that **th**under makes? Can you find a **sh**adow during a rain **sh**ower? If you had the **ch**ance, how would you **ch**ange the weather?

th

Thermometer begins with the consonant digraph **th**. Circle each picture whose name begins with the sound of **th**.

Say the name of each picture. Circle **t** or **th** for each beginning sound. Then print the name on the line. Use the words in the box.

thin	ten	tape	thorn	throne	thumb
thirty	three	toys	tube	think	throw

1 th t

_____

2 th t

_____

3 th t

_____

4 th t

_____

5 **3** th t

_____

6 **10** th t

_____

7 th t

_____

8 th t

_____

9 th t

_____

10 th t

_____

11 **30** th t

_____

12 th t

_____

sh

Shorts begins with the consonant digraph **sh**. Say the name of each picture. Circle the letters for each beginning sound. Then circle the pictures whose names begin with **sh**.

1 **sh** **th**	2 **sh** **th**	3 **sh** **th**	4 **sh** **th**
5 **sh** **th**	6 **sh** **th**	7 **sh** **th**	8 **sh** **th**
9 **sh** **th**	10 **sh** **th**	11 **sh** **th**	12 **sh** **th**
13 **sh** **th**	14 **sh** **th**	15 **sh** **th**	16 **sh** **th**

Say the name of each picture. Circle the name and print it on the line. In the last box, draw a picture of a word whose name begins with the consonant digraph **sh**. Print the word on the line.

1
seed
sad
shed
_____

2
shell
sell
seal
_____

3
shave
save
vase
_____

4
hips
safe
shapes
_____

5
soap
sheep
sleep
_____

6
shop
stop
drop
_____

7
hurt
sort
shirt
_____

8
gift
soft
shelf
_____

9
shoe
hoe
see
_____

10
lake
shake
snake
_____

11
ship
hip
sip
_____

12
_____

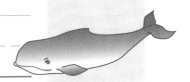

Whale begins with the consonant digraph **wh**. Circle each picture whose name begins with the sound of **wh**.

wh

1	2	3	4
5	6	7	8
		9	10
		11	12

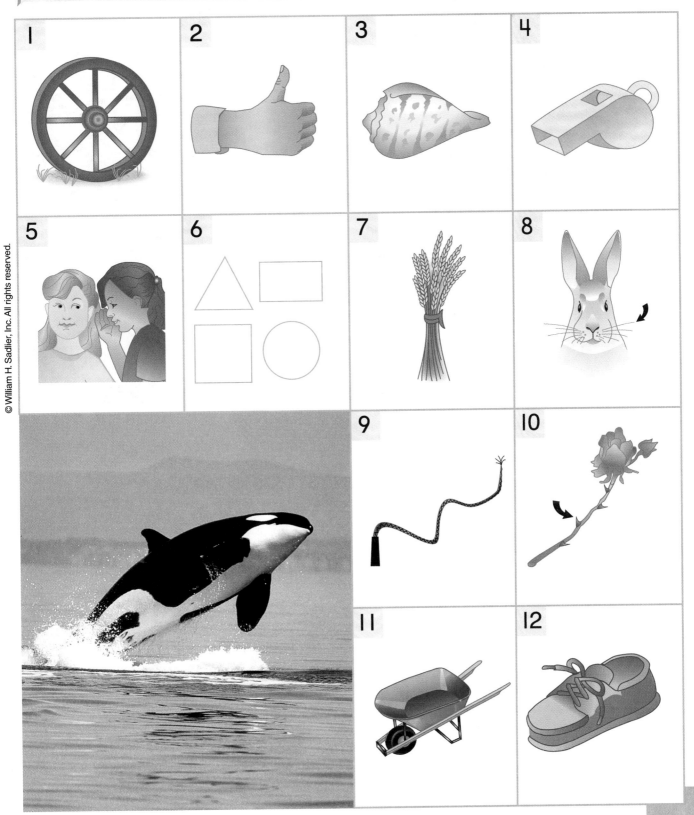

white	What	whipped	When	Why

1. "**What** a bad weather day!"

2. _____ I woke up, it was sunny.

3. Then the _____ clouds turned gray.

4. The wind _____ the leaves back and forth.

5. "_____ does it have to storm?" I whined.

ch

Cherry begins with the consonant digraph **ch**. Circle each picture whose name begins with the sound of **ch**.

1	2	3	4
5	6	7	8
	9	10	
		11	12

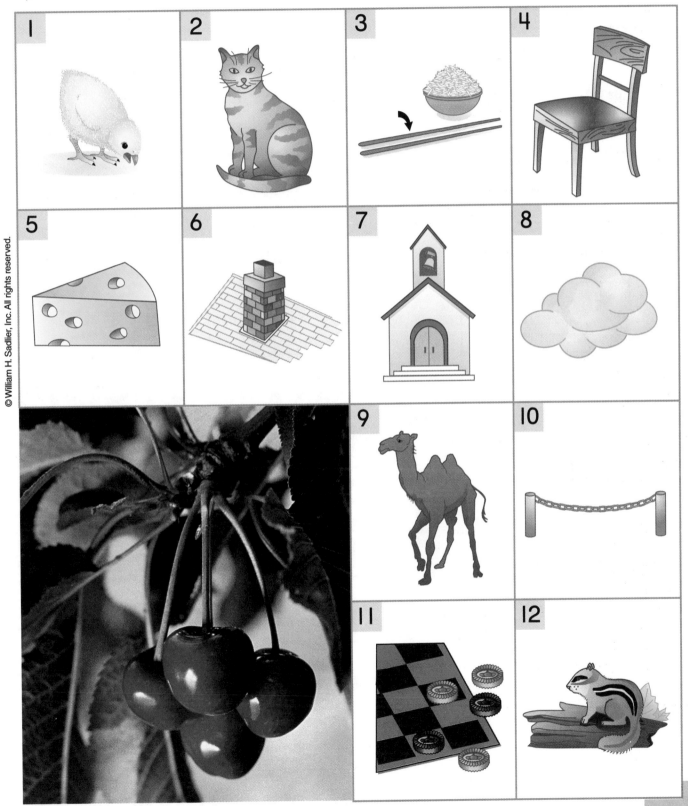

Say the name of each picture. Circle **c** or **ch** for each beginning sound. Then print the name on the line. Use the words in the box.

check	cap	cheek	cape	chin	chop
chalk	cherry	coat	chick	chain	cub

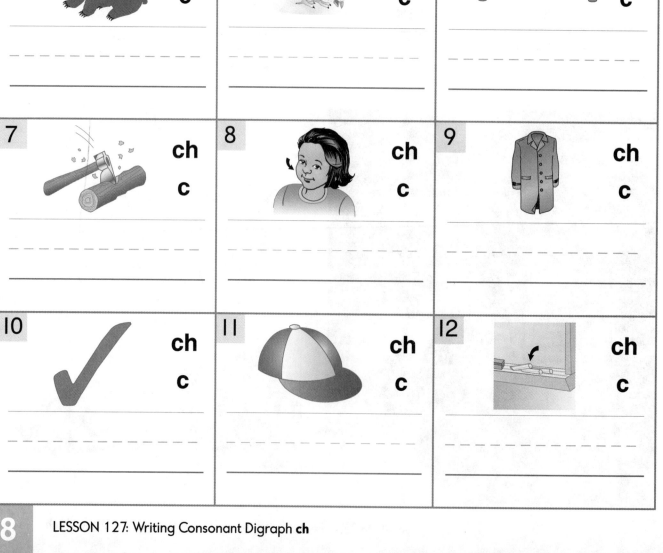

1   ch   c

2   ch   c

3   ch   c

4   ch   c

5   ch   c

6   ch   c

7   ch   c

8   ch   c

9   ch   c

10   ch   c

11   ch   c

12   ch   c

kn

Knee begins with the consonant digraph **kn**. Say the name of each picture. Circle the letters that stand for the beginning sound. Then circle the pictures whose names begin with **kn**.

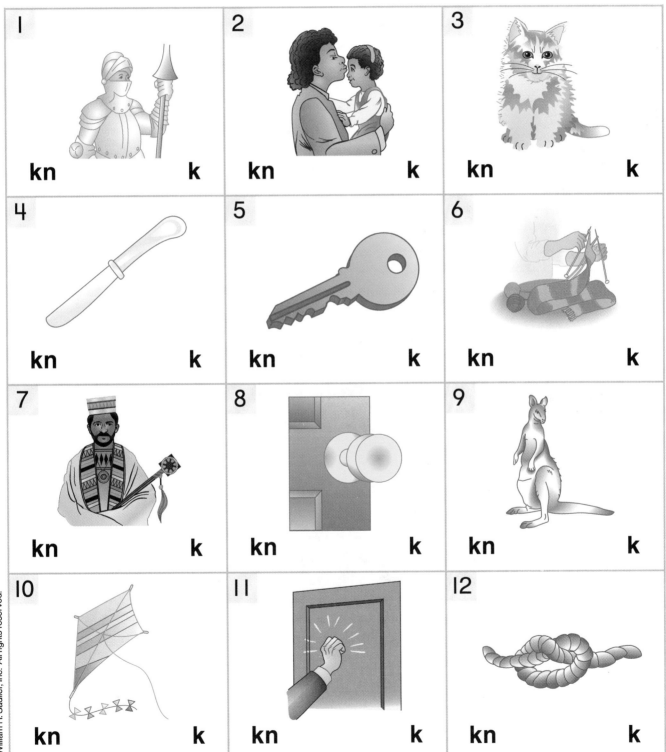

1	2	3
kn **k**	**kn** **k**	**kn** **k**
4	5	6
kn **k**	**kn** **k**	**kn** **k**
7	8	9
kn **k**	**kn** **k**	**kn** **k**
10	11	12
kn **k**	**kn** **k**	**kn** **k**

LESSON 128: Recognizing the Sound of Consonant Digraph **kn**

259

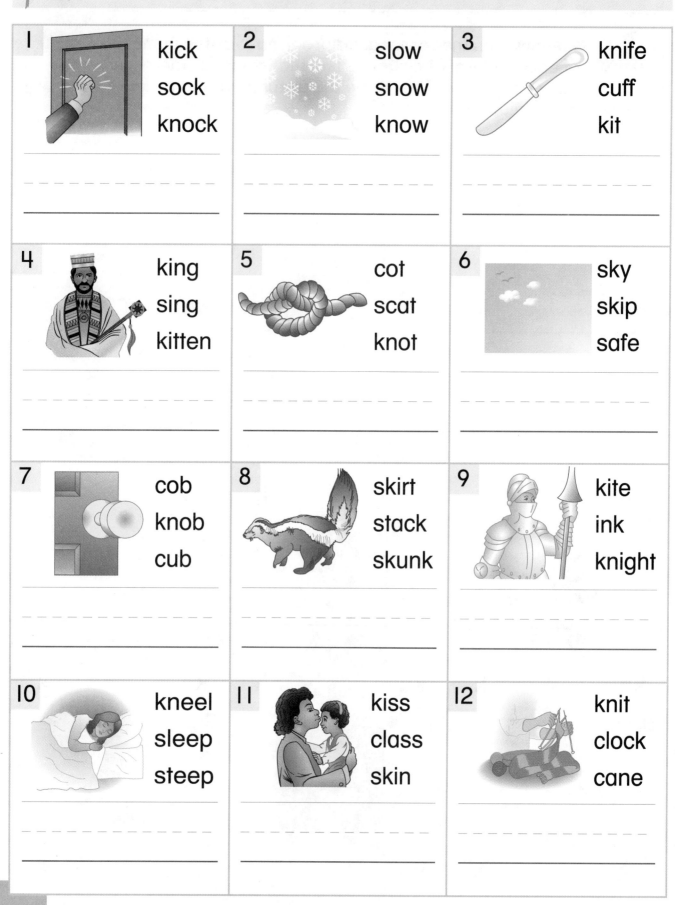

1

kick
sock
knock

2

slow
snow
know

3

knife
cuff
kit

4

king
sing
kitten

5

cot
scat
knot

6

sky
skip
safe

7

cob
knob
cub

8

skirt
stack
skunk

9

kite
ink
knight

10

kneel
sleep
steep

11

kiss
class
skin

12

knit
clock
cane

Spell and Write

Say and spell the words in the box. Then print each word under the digraph in its name. Circle the digraphs in each word.

thing
sheep
white
chain
knob
thin
she
know
three
where
chin
shapes

th

1. (th)ing

2. _____

3. _____

sh

4. _____

5. _____

6. _____

wh

7. _____

8. _____

ch

9. _____

10. _____

kn

11. _____

12. _____

Spell and Write

Pretend you are the pilot of a plane. Write about one of your trips in your pilot's log. Use one or more of your spelling words.

thing
sheep
white
chain
knob
thin
she
know
three
where
chin
shapes

Date: _____

LESSON 129: Connecting Spelling and Writing

Say the name of each picture. Print the letters that stand for the missing digraph on the line. Use **th, sh, wh, ch,** or **kn**.

1 ___orn	2 ___ot	3 ___oe
4 ___ite	5 ___ain	6 **3** ___ree
7 ___ip	8 ___op	9 ___ee
10 ___ale	11 ___ell	12 ___ick

Read the riddles. Print the answers on the lines. The picture clues will help you. Then circle the words with consonant digraphs.

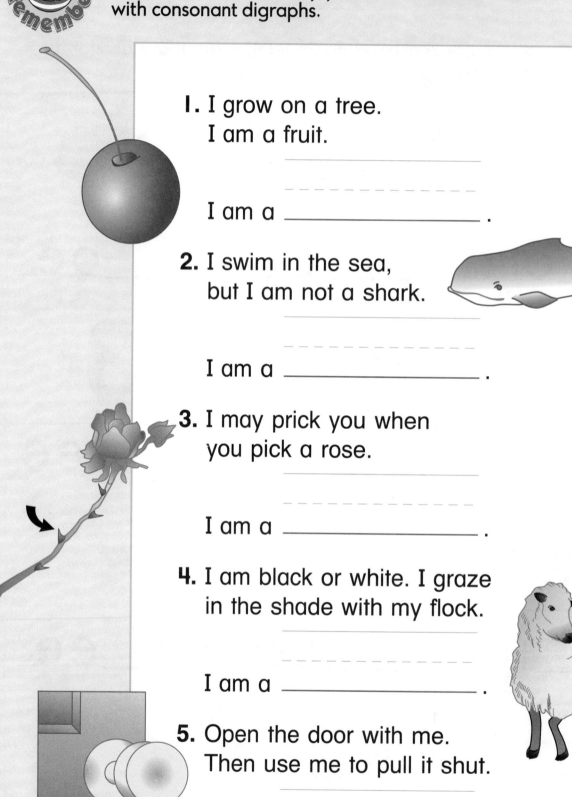

1. I grow on a tree.
I am a fruit.

_____

_ _ _ _ _ _ _ _ _ _ _ _ _

I am a _____ .

2. I swim in the sea,
but I am not a shark.

_____

_ _ _ _ _ _ _ _ _ _ _ _ _

I am a _____ .

3. I may prick you when
you pick a rose.

_____

_ _ _ _ _ _ _ _ _ _ _ _ _

I am a _____ .

4. I am black or white. I graze
in the shade with my flock.

_____

_ _ _ _ _ _ _ _ _ _ _ _ _

I am a _____ .

5. Open the door with me.
Then use me to pull it shut.

_____

_ _ _ _ _ _ _ _ _ _ _ _ _

I am a _____ .

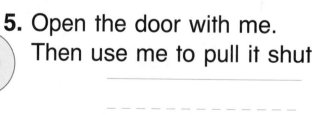
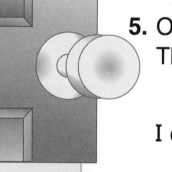

LESSON 130: Reviewing Consonant Digraphs

Look at the pictures. Then read and talk about them.

You know there are many kinds of clouds. They come in different shapes and colors.

Cumulus clouds are white and fluffy. You see them when the sun shines. Cirrus clouds look like feathers. When they are in the sky, the weather may change soon. A layer of stratus clouds can cover the sky. Stratus clouds may be gray. They often bring rain.

When you go outside, look up. What are clouds telling you about the weather?

Cumulus Clouds

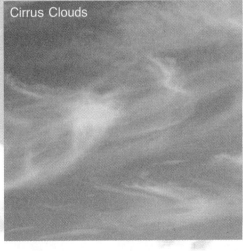

Cirrus Clouds

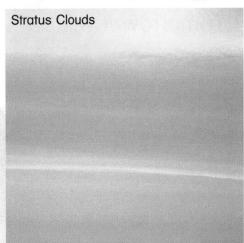

Stratus Clouds

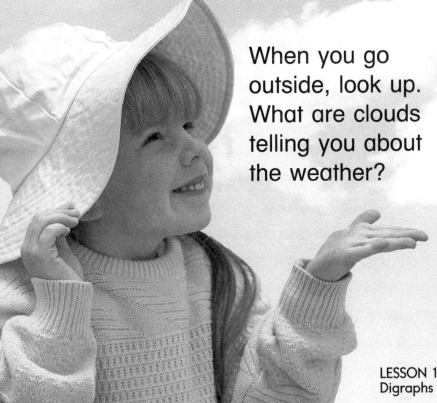

LESSON 131: Words with Consonant
Digraphs in Context

265

Write about and draw a picture of each day's weather. Circle any consonant digraphs you use.

Yesterday it was

_____

_____

Today it is

_____

_____

Tomorrow it will be

_____

_____

LESSON 131: Writing Words with Consonant Digraphs

Look at the consonant digraph at the begining of each row. Then fill in the circles under the pictures whose names begin with the same sound.

1	**wh**				
2	**kn**				
3	**sh**				
4	**th**				
5	**ch**				
6	**wh**				

1

_____

_____

_____ clouds are in the sky.

Thick

Chick

Shoe

2

_____

_____

The clouds are _____ of gray.

wheat

knits

shades

3

_____

_____

I _____ what that means.

show

know

throw

4

_____

_____

The weather will _____ soon.

shave

thin

change

5

_____

_____

_____ will I wear if it is chilly?

What

Chin

Chain

6

_____

_____

I'd better not wear _____ .

three

shell

shorts

TOMMY

I put a seed into the ground
And said, "I'll watch it grow."
I watered it and cared for it
As well as I could know.

One day I walked in my back yard
And oh, what did I see!
My seed had popped itself right out,
Without consulting me.

Gwendolyn Brooks

Critical Thinking
What would you do to help a seed grow?
What kinds of seeds grow into big plants?

LESSON 133: Introduction to Word Structure

Dear Family,

As your child progresses through this unit, you can help phonics come alive at home. Your child will learn about things that grow, and even words that "grow" from other words—contractions, words with endings, and compound words.

● Help your child read the words below. Which words have the **ed** and **ing** endings? Which word comes from **sun** and **flower**? From **I** and **will**?

Ending **ed** Terminación **ed**	Ending **ing** Terminación **ing**
planted	growing

● Read the poem "Tommy" on the reverse side of this page.

● Talk about some of the many things that grow, such as flowers, kittens, trees—and, of course, children.

● Help your child find words in the poem with endings (**watered, cared, walked, popped, consulting**), compound words (**itself, without**), and the contraction **I'll**.

Apreciada Familia:

A medida que los niños avanzan en esta unidad ustedes pueden revivir los fonemas en la casa. Los niños aprenderán sobre el crecimiento de las cosas y algunas palabras que "crecen", contracciones, palabras compuestas y con terminaciones.

● Ayuden al niño a leer estas palabras. ¿Cuáles terminan en **ed** y en **ing**? ¿Cuál palabra vienen de **sun** y **flower**? ¿Cuál viene de **I** y **will**?

Compound Word Palabra Compuesta	Contraction Contracción
sunflower	I'll

● Lean el poema "Tommy" en la página 269.

● Hablen de las cosas que crecen como las flores, las plantas los niños.

● Ayuden a su niño a encontrar palabras con terminación en el poema . (**watered, cared, walked, popped, consulting**), compuestas (**itself, without**) y contracciones, (**I'll**).

PROJECT

Draw a flower on paper and print **ing** in the center. Help your child make the flower "grow" by printing words with that ending in the petals. Draw another flower using the ending **ed**. Use the words in sentences.

PROYECTO

Dibujen una flor y escriban **ing** en el centro. Ayuden a su hijo a hacer "crecer" la flor escribiendo palabras con esa terminación en los pétalos. Dibujen otra flor usando la terminación **ed**. Usen las palabras en oraciones.

Sometimes you can make new words by adding **ed** or **ing** to the base words. Look at each picture and read the base word in Column 1.
Add **ing** to the base word in Column 2.
Add **ed** to the base word in Column 3.

Then use each word in a sentence. Say the sentence aloud.

I **row** the boat. I am **rowing** right now. Yesterday I **rowed** the boat.

Column 1	Column 2	Column 3
Base Word	+ ing	+ ed
1 row	rowing	rowed
2 cook		
3 kick		
4 yell		
5 crawl		

Read the sentence. Circle the ending on the word in dark type. Print the base word on the line.

1   The farmer is **p l a n t （i n g）** a new crop.

   plant

2   The baby duck **q u a c k e d** .

3   Do you like **s l e e p i n g** in a tent?

4   Jess is **b r u s h i n g** the dog now.

5   Keesha **s p i l l e d** the bag of seeds.

6   The leaf **f l o a t e d** down the stream.

Read each sentence. Circle the word that will complete the sentence correctly. Then print the word on the line.

1	I've always _____ a garden.	want wanted wanting
2	One day Mom was _____ seeds.	plant planted planting
3	She _____ me a pack of my own.	hand handed handing
4	I planted corn seeds and _____.	wait waited waiting
5	Soon I _____ something good.	smell smelled smelling
6	Dad was _____ my corn.	cook cooked cooking

Living Things Grow

At first, the baby Toyo crawled,
But soon he could walk.
He was playing and laughing
And learning to talk.

All living things grow up,
Not just me and you.
Seeds, trees, birds, and pups—
They're all growing, too.

_____

1. At first, the baby _____ .

_____

2. Soon he was _____ and laughing.

_____

3. He was _____ to talk.

_____

4. All living things are _____ .

compound word is a word made from two or more shorter words. **Strawberry** is a compound word. Put the two small words together to make a compound word. Print the compound word on the line.

straw + berry = strawberry

1.  sun + flower = _____

2.  foot + ball = _____

3.  rain + coat = _____

4.  wheel + chair = _____

5.  wish + bone = _____

6.  butter + fly = _____

Circle the pictures whose names are compound words.

1 grasshopper	2 playpen	3 shoe	4 shoelace
5 baseball	6 pony	7 backpack	8 flashlight
9 wink	10 wishbone	11 newspaper	12 chopsticks
13 mailbox	14 wheelbarrow	15 watermelon	16 checkers

LESSON 136: Recognizing Compound Words

Join together a word from Box 1 and a word from Box 2 to make a compound word that names each picture. Print the word on the line beside the picture.

Box 1			Box 2		
pop	rain	foot	chair	pack	ball
scare	wheel	back	corn	coat	crow

1. football

2.

3.

4.

5.

6.

1. I am a pack for your books.
I ride on your back.

_____

I am a _____ .

2. I stand in a field and wait for crows.
When a crow comes near, I scare it!

_____

I am a _____ .

3. I am a big yellow flower
that loves to grow in the sun.

_____

I am a _____ .

4. You will stay dry in the rain
if you wear a coat like me.

_____

I am a _____ .

5. When the light goes off,
I'll flash on to help you see.

_____

I am a _____ .

A contraction is a short way of writing two words as one. One or more letters are left out. An apostrophe (') shows where the letters were.

Color each leaf if the contraction stands for the other two words below it.

she + is = she's

I am = I'm   she is = she's   we are = we're
he is = he's   you are = you're
it is = it's   they are = they're

1	2	3
I'm I am	we're I was	you're you are

| 4 | 5 | 6 |
| it's
it is | she's
she did | he's
he is |

| 7 | 8 | 9 |
| she's
she had | they're
they are | you're
you have |

| 10 | 11 | 12 |
| we're
we are | they're
they have | she's
she is |

Contractions can be made with **will** and **not**.
Read the words on the flower petals. Color
the petals with a contraction that is made
from the word in the center of each flower.

he + will =
he'll

is + not =
isn't

I will = I'll   we will = we'll   is not = isn't
he will = he'll   you will = you'll   do not = don't
she will = she'll   they will = they'll   does not=doesn't
it will = it'll   are not = aren't

Spell and Write Say and spell the words in the box. Then print each word under the correct heading.

I'm
she's
they're
doesn't
don't
they'll
it'll
we're
we'll
he's
you're
isn't

Contraction with *am*

1 _____

Contractions with *is*

2 _____

3 _____

Contractions with *are*

4 _____

5 _____

6 _____

Contractions with *will*

7 _____

8 _____

9 _____

Contractions with *not*

10 _____

11 _____

12 _____

 **Spell and Write** Write some things you and your family are planning to do this summer. Use one or more of your spelling words.

I'm	they're	don't	it'll	we'll	you're
she's	doesn't	they'll	we're	he's	isn't

My Summer Plans

LESSON 139: Connecting Spelling and Writing

Look and Learn

Look at the pictures. Then read and talk about them.

All living things grow.
Sunflowers grow.
So do animals like tigers.
You're growing, too. Aren't you?

Try matching the young plants
and animals to the older ones.
How are they the same?
How are they different?
How do they change as they grow?

Look at a baby picture of yourself.
How have you changed?

LESSON 140: Words with Endings, Compound Words,
and Contractions in Context

283

Check-Up In each row, fill in the missing words.

Base Word	+ ing	+ ed
1 sail	sailing	sailed
2 cook		
3		waited
4	raining	
5	planting	
6 mix		
7		yelled
8 jump		

LESSON 140: Assessing Words with Inflectional Endings

Draw a line to connect two words in each box to make a compound word. Print the compound word on the line.

1 rain wish sun coat	**2** sticks robin scare crow
3 pen sticks chop sail	**4** shoe lace ball pack
5 flash light wind nut	**6** base news wheel ball
7 back pack plane chair	**8** news ball wheel paper

1

Our new puppies <u>are</u> <u>not</u> able to walk.

- ○ doesn't
- ○ aren't
- ○ isn't

2

<u>They</u> <u>will</u> be learning soon.

- ○ He'll
- ○ They'll
- ○ They're

3

<u>They</u> <u>are</u> going to get into lots of things.

- ○ They're
- ○ You're
- ○ We'll

4

Then <u>we</u> <u>are</u> going to be busy.

- ○ you're
- ○ they're
- ○ we're

5

Mom says <u>she</u> <u>is</u> going to need our help.

- ○ I'm
- ○ we'll
- ○ she's

6

<u>It</u> <u>is</u> going to be fun.

- ○ It's
- ○ Isn't
- ○ He's

7

I <u>do</u> <u>not</u> want to miss the fun.

- ○ can't
- ○ you're
- ○ don't

Name _____

STUDENT SKILLS
ASSESSMENT CHECKLIST

☑ Assessed   ☒ Retaught   ■ Mastered

Unit 1 **Auditory Discrimination**
- ❏ Discriminate Initial Consonant Sounds
- ❏ Discriminate Rhyming Sounds

Unit 2 **Letter Recognition and Consonant Sounds**
- ❏ Initial Consonant **f**
- ❏ Initial Consonant **m**
- ❏ Initial Consonant **s**
- ❏ Identify Final Consonants **f, m, s**
- ❏ Initial Consonant **t**
- ❏ Initial Consonant **h**
- ❏ Initial Consonant **b**
- ❏ Identify Final Consonants **t** and **b**
- ❏ Consonants **f, m, s, t, h, b**
- ❏ Initial Consonant **l**
- ❏ Initial Consonant **d**
- ❏ Initial Consonant **c**
- ❏ Identify Final Consonants **l** and **d**
- ❏ Initial Consonant **n**
- ❏ Initial Consonant **g**
- ❏ Initial Consonant **w**
- ❏ Identify Final Consonants **n** and **g**
- ❏ Consonants **l, d, c, n, g, w**
- ❏ Initial Consonant **p**
- ❏ Initial Consonant **r**
- ❏ Initial Consonant **k**
- ❏ Identify Final Consonants **p, r, k**
- ❏ Initial Consonant **j**
- ❏ Initial Consonant **q**

- ❑ Initial Consonant **v**
- ❑ Initial Consonant **x**
- ❑ Initial Consonants **y** and **z**
- ❑ Consonants **p, r, k, j, q, v, x, y, z**
- ❑ Recognize and Write Medial Consonants
- ❑ Initial, Medial, Final Consonants

Unit 3 Short Vowels

- ❑ Short Vowel **a**
- ❑ Short Vowel **i**
- ❑ Short Vowel **o**
- ❑ Short Vowel **u**
- ❑ Short Vowel **e**

Unit 4 Long Vowels

- ❑ Long Vowel **a**
- ❑ Long Vowel **i**
- ❑ Long Vowel **o**
- ❑ Long Vowel **u**
- ❑ Long Vowel **e**
- ❑ Final **y** as a Vowel

Unit 5 Consonant Blends

- ❑ L Blends
- ❑ R Blends
- ❑ S Blends
- ❑ Final Consonant Blends

Unit 6 Consonant Digraphs

- ❑ Consonant Digraphs **th, sh, wh, ch, kn**

Unit 7 Word Structure

- ❑ Inflectional Endings **-ed** and **-ing**
- ❑ Compound Words
- ❑ Contractions

Good Books
Make Good Friends

1

3

on the ranch or in the sea.

Fold

Fold

Draw a picture of a book
you would like to share.

8

Fun adventures, silly rhymes!

6

Directions: Help your child cut and fold the book. Read it together
several times. Help your child identify the rhyming words.

UNIT 1: Take-home Book

289

I have good times. I make new friends.

I'm never bored. I feel so free

Fold

Fold

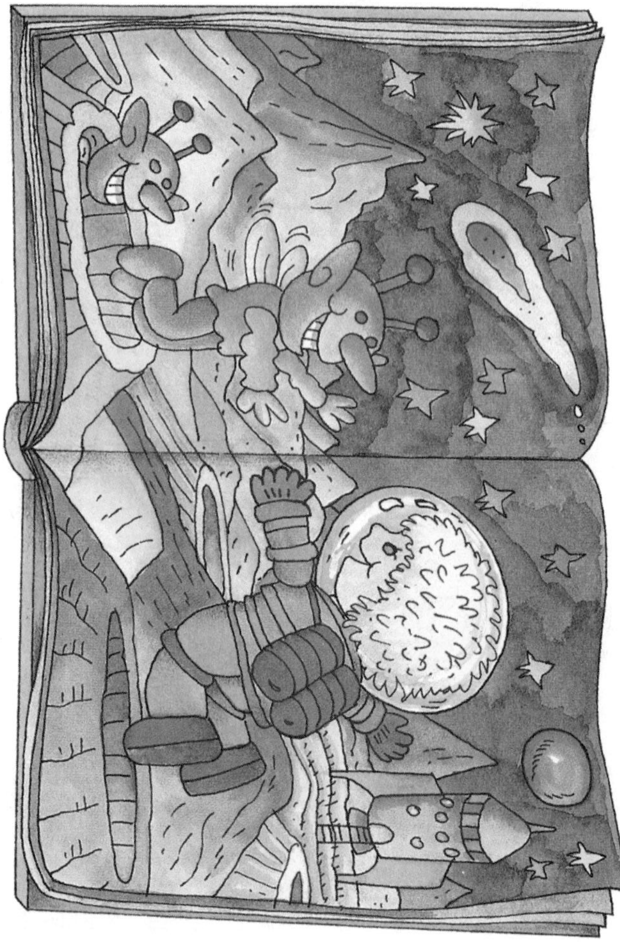

I never want the books to end.

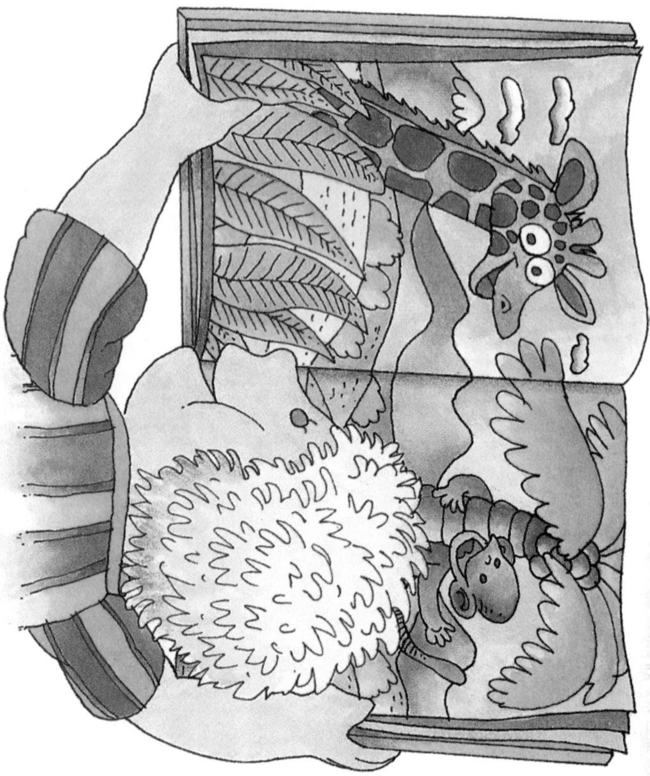

Good books, good times!

UNIT 1: Take-home Book

Name _____

I LOVE PARADES

Fold

3

with quick stepping clowns,

Fold

and me!
Draw a picture to show
what you do in the parade.

8

razzle dazzle floats,

6

Directions: Help your child cut and fold the book. Read it together
and talk about the pictures. Can you find a word that starts with
each beginning consonant?

UNIT 2: Take-home Book

4

very noisy bands,

Fold

2

I love to see parades

Fold

kicking, jumping zebras,

5

huge, gray elephants

7

UNIT 2: Take-home Book

Is It a Bug?

It will grow up to be a moth.

A lion, a fish, and a bear—all are bugs.
Were you surprised?

8

Fold

Is a lion a bug?

An ant lion is.

3

Fold

A silverfish bends like a fish in a pond.
It snacks on books or rugs.

6

Directions: Help your child cut and fold the book. As you read together, pause before turning the page to guess what will be on the next page. How many short vowel words can you find?

UNIT 3: Take-home Book

4

An ant lion digs a pit to make a trap. It gobbles up bugs that drop in.

2

What is a bug?

I bet you'll be surprised.

Is a fish a bug?

A silverfish is.

5

Is a bear a bug?

A woolybear is.

7

Name _____

We Can Take Care of the Earth

We can clean up a stream.
We can plant trees beside it.

3

— Fold —

— Fold —

President of the United States
The White House
Washington, DC 20005

We can learn the rules and tell what we know. We can write to someone who can help.

8

We can turn off the water while we brush our teeth.

6

Directions: Help your child cut and fold the book. Read the book together and talk about how your family helps the environment. Find long vowel words.

UNIT 4: Take-home Book

295

We can try to save paper. We can take bags to the grocery store.

See how the earth looks. It doesn't look nice. What can we do?

Fold

Fold

We can be sure to turn off the lights when we go outside.

5

RECYCLING SALE

PUZZLE

We can recycle used toys. We can give them away or have a sale.

7

Making Sense

Name _____

1

3

What sounds loud?

What smells good?

It looks _____

It feels _____

It is a _____

8

6

Directions: Help your child cut and fold the book. Read it together and talk about the questions. Find words that have blends, like **grapes, plane, smells,** and **pond.**

UNIT 5: Take-home Book

297

4

What tastes best?

2

What looks blue?

Fold

Fold

What feels soft?

What is this?
Print your guess on the next page.

5

7

UNIT 5: Take-home Book

3

WEATHER CHANGES

Name _____

Fold

Fold

Weather changes.
Storms dash by.
Once again
It's warm and dry.

Thunder's knocking.
Crash and flash!
Rain is swishing.
Splash! Splash!

8

9

Directions: Help your child cut and fold the book. Read the poem together and look at the pictures. Talk about how weather changes where you live and how to stay safe during a storm. What words can you find that have the letters **sh**, **th**, **ch**, **wh**, and **kn**?

UNIT 6: Take-home Book

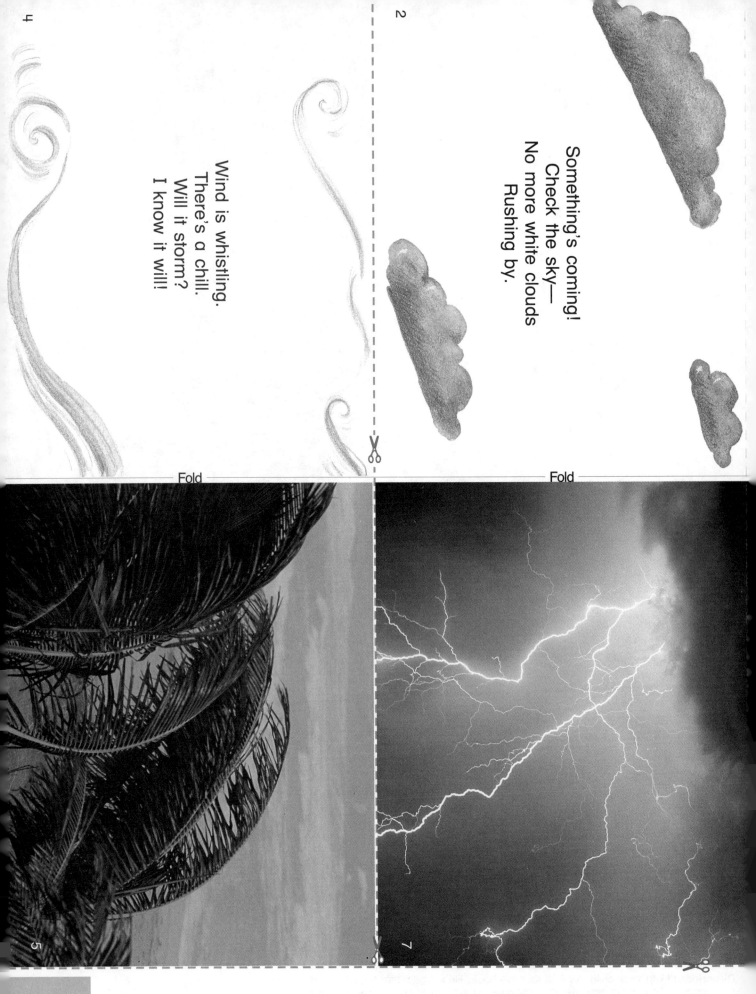

4

Wind is whistling.
There's a chill.
Will it storm?
I know it will!

2

Something's coming!
Check the sky—
No more white clouds
Rushing by.

Fold

Fold

5

7

UNIT 6: Take-home Book

Name _____

Planting Seeds

3

Tim has gathered these things:
a paper cup, markers, soil, grass seed.

— Fold —

— Fold —

He has placed the cup in the light.
He will be watering it soon.

8

Tim is pouring soil into the cup.

9

Directions: Help your child cut and fold the book. As you read
together, try to predict what Tim will make. Look for words with
ed and **ing** endings.

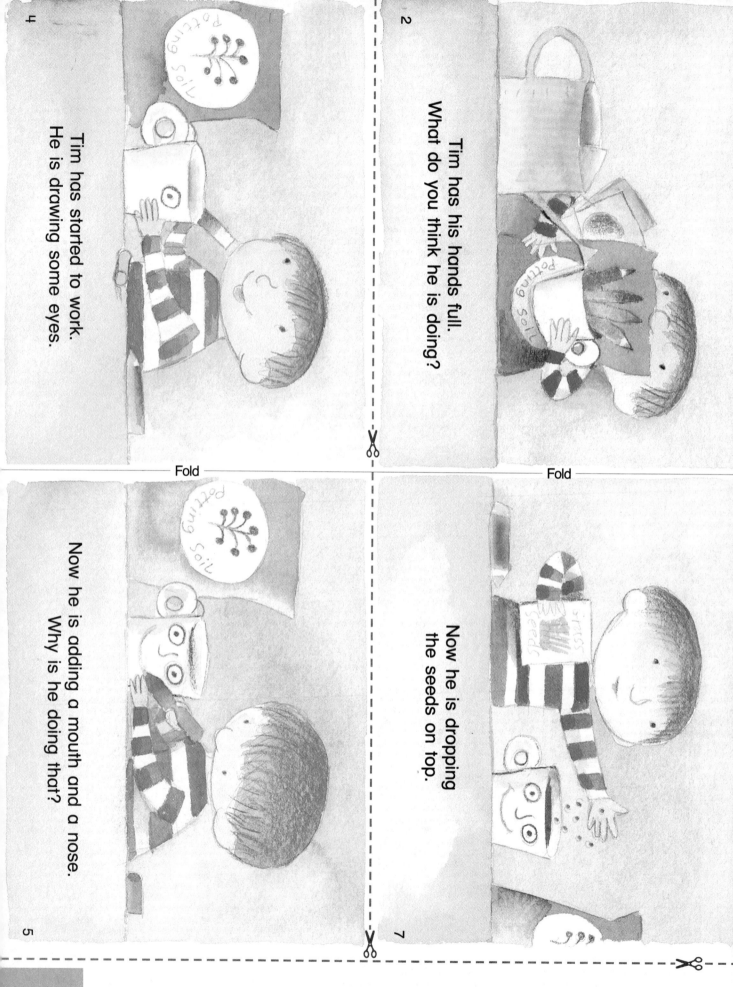

4

Tim has started to work.
He is drawing some eyes.

2

Tim has his hands full.
What do you think he is doing?

Now he is adding a mouth and a nose.
Why is he doing that?

5

Now he is dropping
the seeds on top.

7

Name _____

Aren't You Something!

3

Your family and friends came to see you.
Everyone said, "Isn't the baby cute?"

Some day you'll be a grownup.
Draw a picture of what you'll do then.

8

You grew big enough to go to school.
Everybody said, "It's time to learn
and have fun!"

6

Directions: Help your child cut and fold the book. Read the story
together and talk about things your child did as a baby and toddler.
Then find contractions and compound words in the text and pictures.

UNIT 7: Take-home Book

303

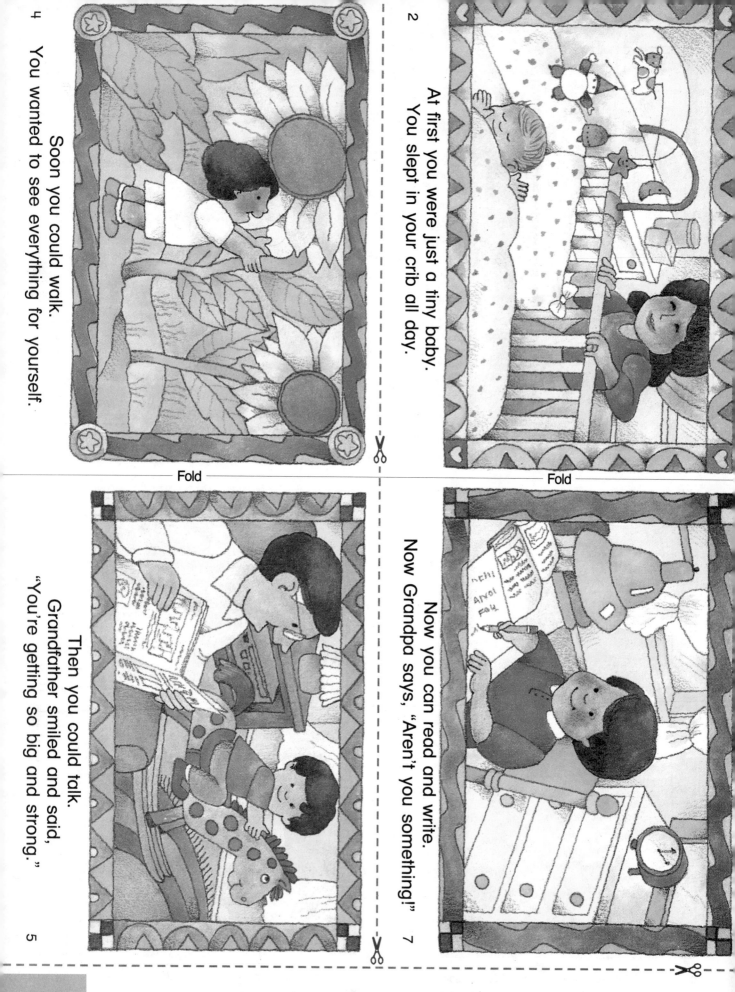

4

Soon you could walk.
You wanted to see everything for yourself.

2

At first you were just a tiny baby.
You slept in your crib all day.

5

Then you could talk.
Grandfather smiled and said,
"You're getting so big and strong."

7

Now you can read and write.
Now Grandpa says, "Aren't you something!"

A B C D

E F G H

I J K L

M N O P

Q R S T

U V W X

Y Z a e

i o u a